ERICA WILSON'S
KNITTING BOOK

Charles Scribner's Sons   New York

Charles Scribner's Sons
Macmillan Publishing Company
866 Third Avenue, New York, NY 10022
Collier Macmillan Canada, Inc.

Macmillan books are available at special discounts for bulk purchases for sales promotions, premiums, fund-raising, or educational use. For details, contact:

Special Sales Director
Macmillan Publishing Company
866 Third Avenue
New York, NY 10022

Erica Wilson's Knitting Book
Editors: Dale Jagemann, Sandy Towers
Design: Viola Andrycich
Photography: Vladimir Kagan: pages 1, 43, 44–56, 65; Mark Hamilton: Closeups, pages 1–65; Lilo Raymond: pages 13, 153; Vanessa Kagan: page 35; Robin Wools: pages 82, 83, 86, 98, 154, 160, 163, 166
Technique Illustrations: Heidi Lang, Gill Schneck, Marsha Moore, Donna Rothchild, and the author
Models: Vanessa Kagan, Pamela Paspa, Skipper Willauer, Anne Lingemann, and Emmy Higgins
Historical photographs: The Cooper-Hewitt Museum Library, Smithsonian Institution, Art Resource, New York: Fileuses de Sondernach from *A Travers L'Alsage et La Lorraine,* page 6; Needlework Tools from *History of Needlework Tools,* page 7; *The Stocking Knitter* by Annibale Caracci (1560–1609) from *The History of Needlework,* page 7; The Chinese Stocking-Maker from the Far East, page 8; Origin of Stocking Frame from *Knitted Fabrics,* Quilter, page 9; The First Frame-Made Stocking from *Knitted Fabrics,* Quilter, page 9; Three Fishermen in Stocks from *Patterns for Guernseys,* Thompson, page 10; Florence silk gloves from *Florence Home Needlework,* page 11; Young Englishman painted by Nicholas Hilliard, Victoria and Albert Museum, London, page 11. The Metropolitan Museum of Art, page 9: Jacket, purchase 1914 the Cooper-Hewitt Fund, and Waistcoat, the Fletcher Fund, 1946.

Photographs of the children's sweaters on pages 82, 83, 86, 98, 154, 160, 163, and 166 are courtesy of Robin Wools, Emu International, Great Britain.

My grateful thanks to the following people for patterns and instructions: Anny Blatt sweaters on pages 76, 96, 114, 121, 144, and 150; the Sheepish Grin on page 102; Robin Wools, Emu International, Great Britain, on pages 82, 83, 86, 98, 154, 160, 163, and 166; Lorna Boquest, page 132; and Leslie Robertson, page 66; Lion Brand Yarns, pages 70, 108, and 127. The sweaters on pages 70, 108, and 127 were designed by the author and have appeared in *Family Circle* magazine; the sweater on page 148 was designed by the author for *Vogue Knitting Magazine.*

Library of Congress Cataloging-in-Publication Data
Wilson, Erica
[Knitting book]
Erica Wilson's Knitting book.
 p. cm.
ISBN 0-684-18561-X
I. Knitting—Patterns. I. Title. II. Title:Knitting book.
TT820.W598 1988
746.9'2—dc19   87-15894

10 9 8 7 6 5 4 3 2 1

Printed in the United States of America

CONTENTS

4

INTRODUCTION

So that you can learn techniques and apply them to any sweater, this book is divided into four sections.

The first section, "Texture," shows how a sweater in one color can have drama—because of raised patterns, openwork lace, or three-dimensional sculptural effects.

Combining texture and color gives you yet another dimension. A third technique, color changing, is when you carry yarns of different colors across the row at the back of the work, bringing each one to the front as you need it. Called *intarsia,* this can turn your sweater into a work of art, with all the verve of an impressionist painting. Or it can be used to make overall repeat patterns like a jacquard fabric, creating kaleidoscopes of color.

When you finally take needle in hand to add decorative stitches on top of your finished knitting, you will realize that the possibilities are unlimited.

Once you have followed some of the techniques shown here letter-for-letter, you will feel bold enough to try out your own ideas. Use the special section and knitter's graph paper at the end of this book to create unique sweaters of your own design.

THE HISTORY OF KNITTING

As well as being one of the most ancient of crafts, knitting is probably the one most taken for granted. No other fabric can rival the warmth and elasticity of a knitted cap, shirt, or stocking. So knitted garments were made to be used, and few ancient relics have been preserved. But knitting probably goes back before recorded history. The Anglo-Saxon verb *cnytte,* meaning "to join, fasten, or fuse with knotting," was in use by A.D. 1000, according to the *Oxford English Dictionary.* Bones were said to "knit" together, fruit "knit" on the tree branches, and even brows were "knit." "Knit hosen" were common, and the *Oxford English Dictionary* quotes a 1603 reference to "a paire of sleeves of gold and silver knytt."

The earliest knitters were probably Arabian shepherds, who knitted on foot as they guarded their flocks, using materials familiar to them: wooden sticks from trees or shrubs and wool spun from the fleece. In the interests of speed (and because this method is easier when standing up), one needle was stuck in the waistband, leaving the hands free to manipulate the yarn and the needle. Interestingly enough, some knitters in Spain and in the Fair Isles use this method even today. Knitting in the round with three, four, or five needles has perhaps even earlier origins. We know that caps with no seams date back at least to Coptic Egypt of the fourth and fifth centuries.

Because clothing made of knitted wool insulated the wearer from heat and cold, it was used by sailors, who spread the knowledge of knitting to all the ports they visited. *The Bayeux Tapestry,* which depicts the invasion of England by William the Conqueror in 1066, illustrates soldiers wearing horizontally striped hose that must have been knitted.

The story goes that in the sixteenth century, when the Spanish armada was wrecked around the shores of England, Scotland, and Ireland, Spanish

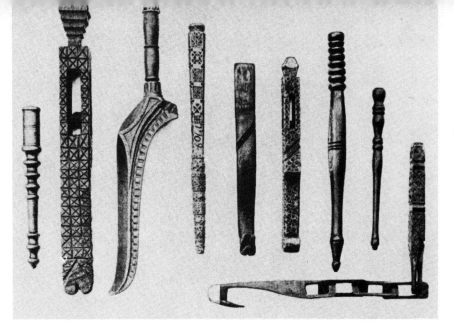

Hooks and sheaths to hold knitting "pins" as the work was being done. See page 14.

Women in native regional dress spinning and knitting in Alsace, France. A sixteenth-century reference to "Spynsters, Carders, and Cappe Knitters" suggests that women were traditionally the spinners, while men made stockings. If men made stockings at this time, the stockings were chiefly for men to wear. The husbands of the women in this picture would have worn long knitted stockings with their maroon jackets with silver buttons, black waistcoats, gray culottes, and buckled shoes.

The Stocking Knitter, by Annibale Caracci. An itinerant Italian stocking-maker of the sixteenth century plying his trade as he looks for a possible customer. Notice the board slung on his hip with two fixed barrels for holding the different-colored threads with which he is working.

sailors who were rescued taught their art of knitting to the inhabitants. The duke of Medina-Sidonia himself—leader of the armada—was wrecked on the Fair Isles, where the tradition of patterned knitting has been handed down for generations.

The sixteenth century brought about a revolution in knitting, chiefly because of the invention of that ubiquitous modern garment, the silk stocking. Until that time, thick leggings of quilted material, or rather homely fabric, were the only ways of keeping warm and waterproof. "She hobbles as she goes, With her blanket hose, Her shoon smeared with tallow."

By the sixteenth century in Italy, the itinerant stocking maker was already a familiar figure. The historian John Stow tells us that the first pair of worsted stockings knitted in England were made in the reign of Elizabeth I by William Rider, who plied his trade at the foot of London Bridge and who copied a pair of Italian hose from Mantua and presented them to the earl of Pembroke.

Silken hose from Italy provoked a furor in fashion, and Queen Elizabeth is said to be the first woman in the world to have owned a pair.

A clergyman named William Lee, whose wife had a successful hand-knit stocking shop, watched her at her craft and invented a machine for the production of worsted stockings. After three years his machine was perfected, and he applied to Queen Elizabeth for the exclusive rights to produce it. But this she refused, saying it would take a living away from hand-knitters, many of whom were ladies of her court. Disappointed, Lee went to France, where Henry IV entertained him and would have become his patron. Before this could happen, however, Henry IV was assassinated,

Chinese stocking-maker quilting fabric

and Lee was thrown in prison for being a Protestant. He later died in Paris, brokenhearted and penniless, although his knitting frame was the basis of the machine that ultimately fathered the whole industry of knitted fabrics.

By the late sixteenth century, knitting had become an art, as is made amply clear by the patterned violet, gold, and white silk cushion found in the tomb of Fernando de la Cerda in Castille, Spain. By that time, knitting had become so established that guilds were set up to control what was becoming a very popular and remunerative form of fabric construction. In those days, men, far from considering knitting women's work, served apprenticeships of six years in order to earn the right to call themselves masters of the craft.

The high level of skill that professional knitters in Europe were expected to exhibit can be seen in the masterpieces apprentices were required to execute to complete their course of study. Apprentices had only thirteen weeks to work four pieces for review by the guild: a carpet, beret, shirt, and pair of hose. The carpets alone measured approximately 6 feet by 5 feet (2 meters by 1.7 meters), and many were as full of detail and color as woven Persian carpets.

Rigid rules surrounded the production and acceptance of masterpieces. First, color designs were submitted for preliminary approval, the apprentice taking an oath that the designs were his own work. Once the designs were approved, the apprentice was informed of the workshop wherein he had to make all four of the appointed works. If the work was acceptable, he was finally received as a member of the guild and a master craftsman.

William Lee designing his knitting machine

The first silk stocking made by machine being presented to his wife by William Lee

Brocade knitting

Jacket, knitted; embroidered with green and gold trim. Italian, Balkan, seventeenth century.

Waistcoat: undervestment for armor; knitted in purple and gold silk with large floral design. Italian, Venice, sixteenth century.

With the introduction of silk from China, knitting standards became even higher. A new kind of elegance began to appear in knitted fabrics, which often resembled brocades. Gold and silver thread were used, and many exquisite pieces were worked for the royalty of Europe.

On stockings, mittens, bonnets, coats, scarves, and fichus, the variety of stitch patterns grew. One knitting sampler still in existence contains 150 patterns and is not bound off—indicating that the knitter intended to add still more patterns. Work of gossamer fineness is still being created in the Shetland Islands, where soft, lacy baby shawls are made, so light and warm that the tradition is unlikely to die. One test of fineness was to draw a 36-inch (90-centimeter) oval shawl through a wedding ring. Many Shetland knitters can produce two hundred stitches a minute, which explains how it is possible to create such masterpieces in a reasonable amount of time.

During the eighteenth century, beads began to play an important part in knitting. Bead-knitted evening bags were stylish in European courts. For

9

The traditional fisherman's sweater was knitted in different patterns in natural, undyed wool in the Channel Islands, Fair Isles, the Hebrides, the Aran Islands, Skye, and the Isle of Man. In fact, in Europe the word sweater *is seldom used—the garment is called a* jersey *after the Channel island most famous for its production. At one time, the islanders were so occupied with their knitting that agriculture was neglected. A law was passed that anyone found knitting at harvesttime would be put in the stocks and fed only bread and water!*

these bags, fine shadings of color were used to create designs so detailed they were like miniature paintings. Figures and objects alike were depicted with beads and yarn. It is almost certain that the graceful, elegant work of the period was done mainly by women. Embroidery and traditional lace were often added to a knitted base fabric. Many of the pieces found in museums today are marvels of complexity and design.

The early nineteenth century spelled the beginning of the end of hand-knitting as an industry. It was replaced by the machines of the Industrial Revolution. Knitting existed as a cottage industry, however, well into the twentieth century. Indeed, in areas well known for their knitting, such as the Aran and Shetland Islands, knitting as an industry has never died out.

In recent years, a great worldwide renaissance of knitting has taken place. If art is something people engage in for pleasure and not out of necessity, then knitting has finally achieved the status of an art form. It is "wearable art," both creative and practical. Women (and men as well) now practice knitting as a form of self-expression. The wealth of knitting patterns and yarns now commonly available would astound knitters of earlier generations. Today, jewel tones of cotton, silk, and angora; muted shades of cashmere, mohair, and alpaca; and new textures and colors in man-made fibers all inspire creativity, just like the paints of an artist's palette.

For the Renaissance man, the ruff, padded doublet, and the very short breeches were all designed to set off a comely leg clad in skintight knitted silken hose. Often scented and magnificently colored, created by Italian artists and refined by English taste, these stockings were worn only by the very rich because they were very expensive. Besides stockings, the counterpart for women was the shift, often knitted in the finest of silks, sometimes black with gold metallic thread in fine jacquard designs. Lucrezia Borgia owned two hundred of them. Bodices were daringly slashed to allow the shift to show through.

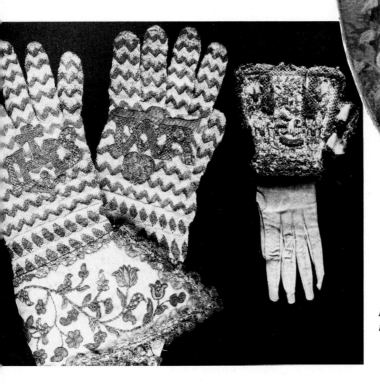

Bishops' gloves: red silk and gold metallic thread, Italy, seventeenth century.

YARNS AND FIBERS

All yarns, whether linen, silk, or cotton, are first spun into a single strand, called a *ply*. This one-ply strand is then twisted together with others for strength: hence two-, three-, or four-ply yarn. Short fibers produce a rough, "homespun"-textured yarn, while long, wavy fibers yield a soft, luxurious one.

Today, the most wonderful array of knitting wools is available to the knitter. Luxurious mohair, cashmere, angora, silk, and cotton mingle with textured yarns in different combinations, some with the sparkle of metallics, some with acrylics for washability and shape. Many expensive yarns in exquisite color ranges have been duplicated in acrylics. These yarns are carefree and much less expensive, but with proper handling, "real" fibers will outlive them. (See "Blocking and Caring for Your Sweater," beginning on page 170.)

Many hand-dyed and specialty yarns are sold in hanks. You must wind them into balls before you begin to knit. This should be done carefully, as tightly wound yarns tend to lose their elasticity. If you wind balls so that the end pulls from the inside, it not only avoids stretching the yarn but prevents the ball from rolling away as you knit. Begin by making a small tube the thickness of one or two fingers from heavy paper or light cardboard. Tape an end of yarn to the tube and begin rolling yarn around it, crisscrossing as you wind. At the end, draw out the cardboard tube and pull the end of yarn. It will continue to come out from the center.

A small, table-attached wool winder is available that will quickly do this work for you. If you use it in combination with a "swift," you can wind several skeins of color and texture together at one time, thereby making your own twisted yarn. A soft mohair, for instance, can be enhanced with a twist of fine mercerized silk to give it a glimmer, or you could combine two or three strands of the same thickness of yarn in different shades to make your own tweed mixture.

It is combining colors and textures that gives knitting its excitement today. When you choose a yarn, make certain that you have enough to complete the garment because dye lots change and the odds are against your finding more of the same color if you should run out.

Generally speaking, the finer the yarn, the more of it you will use. But from knitter to knitter, there is a tremendous variation in the amount of wool needed, depending on your tension—whether you knit tightly or loosely. The question most often asked is, "How do I decide how much *I* will need?" The answer is to go by yardage rather than by weight. One yard of cotton is usually heavier than one yard of wool of the same thickness. For this reason, and also because some of the fancy new yarns look completely different when knitted than in the skein, knitting a sample swatch before you begin is strongly recommended. By multiplication, you can then figure out how many yards

your own knitting tension will require. (See page 33 for more information about gauge.)

To give you some guidelines, here are the basic yarn-weight categories with some average measurements:

Generous Amounts for a Woman's Medium-Sized, Long-Sleeved Pullover (With No Pattern Stitches)

Finger-ing:	(fine baby yarn)	1,600 yards (1,477 meters)
Sport:	(light to medium weight)	1,400 yards (1,292 meters)
Worsted:	(medium to heavy weight)	1,200 yards (1,108 meters)
Bulky:	(very heavy weight)	1,000 yards (923 meters)

If the yarn label gives some measurements only in meters, remember as a rough guide that there are approximately 110 yards to every 100 meters of yarn.

If your pattern recommends one needle size and the yarn you have chosen suggests another, choose the one the pattern specifies to arrive at the right gauge. Also, if your pattern suggests, for example, sport-weight yarn, think carefully about the consequences of using worsted weight instead. Be sure to check gauge!

Yarn Winder

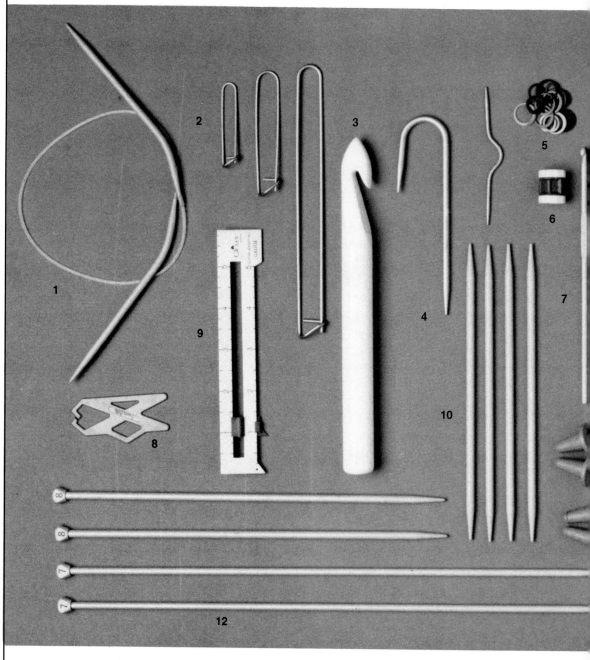

TOOLS

Left to right, top:
1 Circular needles; **2** Stitch holders; **3** Jumbo crochet hook, similar in size to broomstick lace pins; available in sizes 17, 19, 35, and 50; **4** Curved and straight cable needles; **5** Stitch-count markers; **6** Row counter; **7** Crochet hook; **8** Yarn bobbin; **9** Gauge ruler; **10** Double-pointed needles; **11** Point protectors; **12** Knitting needles—short and long.

Needle sizes (American) with their metric equivalents (in parentheses)—0 (2¼), 1 (2¾), 2 (3), 3 (3¼), 4 (3¾), 5 (4½), 6 (4½), 7 (5), 8 (5½), 9 (6), 10 (6½), 10½ (7), 11 (7½), 12 (8), 13 (9), 15 (10)

KNITTING NEEDLES may be long or short, depending on the article to be knitted. They come in pairs in a wide range of thicknesses. The thicker the needles, the larger the size. The size to use is determined by the kind of yarn and the tension of your knitting. Most yarn labels suggest the needle size, but the average sizes to use with the different weights of yarn are:

Fingering:	1, 2*, 3
Sport:	3, 4, 5*
Worsted:	6, 7, 8*
Bulky:	9, 10½*, 11, and up

CIRCULAR NEEDLES are short needles connected by a nylon line or cable, enabling you to knit around and around to create a seamless tube. They can be used only when the number of stitches is sufficient to reach from one needle point to the other. Cable lengths range from 16 to 29 inches (40 to 72.5 centimeters). Sizes are not marked on circular needles; however, needle sizes are the same as straight-needle sizes.

DOUBLE-POINTED NEEDLES come in sets of four or five. Since they are pointed at each end, you can knit tubes that would be too small for circular needles, such as cuffs and necklines. Double-pointed needles come in two lengths, 7 inches and 10 inches (17.5 centimeters and 25 centimeters).

CABLE NEEDLES are double-pointed needles that hold the "waiting" stitches of a cable that are to be knitted in reverse order. The small dip in the center or the curved end cleverly prevents the stitches from sliding off, yet the stitches can be knitted from either side.

*Average needle size

STITCH HOLDERS resemble large safety pins. They are used for holding stitches that will be knitted later.

ROW COUNTERS are small gauges placed on straight needles to keep track of the number row you are knitting.

CROCHET HOOKS come in various sizes. They are useful in knitting for picking up dropped stitches and for finishing, joining, or edging.

STITCH-COUNT MARKERS are small beads placed on a needle to remind a knitter to make an adjustment of some kind. They are especially useful for signaling the end of each round when knitting on circular needles.

GAUGE RULERS are clear plastic rulers marked with inches and stitch shapes. They are used to measure the number of rows and stitches you are getting to the inch (or centimeter) in order to establish gauge.

BROOMSTICK LACE PINS are sold as single needles for use with one finer needle in lace knitting or with bulky yarn.

POINT PROTECTORS are rubber ends to place on needle points in order to prevent stitches from falling off.

TAPESTRY NEEDLES have blunt points. They are useful for joining seams because, unlike sharp-pointed sewing needles, they will not split yarn.

YARN BOBBINS are small spools used in multiple-color knitting. Each carries a different color of yarn. The bobbins are designed to dangle free from the work and prevent the yarns from tangling (see page 125).

CHOOSING YOUR NEEDLES

When you knit, you are creating a fabric. You can make flat, shaped pieces of this fabric and seam them to make a garment, or you can create the garment as you go, knitting "tubes," which will make the finished piece completely seamless. This older method of knitting can be done on sets of double-pointed needles, on spools, on a frame, or even on two straight needles. But it is easiest of all on circular needles.

Circular needles are made from a pair of short needles of any size connected by a heavy plastic line or cable that holds the stitches as you knit around. Depending on what section of the garment you are knitting, the length of the plastic cable needed varies. If the cable is too long, the stitches will stretch as they go around from one point to the other. If it is too short, your stitches will be too crowded.

When you knit on straight needles, you turn your work at the end of every row, knitting first with the "face," or right side, toward you, and then the reverse. To obtain the basic smooth effect of stockinette stitch (known in Europe simply as stocking stitch), you must knit one row and purl the next. This gives one smooth side and one side with wavy ridges. When you knit in the round, either on circular needles or on double-pointed needles, you can knit around and around without changing stitches to produce the same effect. It is easy to see that this must have been the original way of making stockings—hence "stockinette stitch." When you experiment with using circular needles and

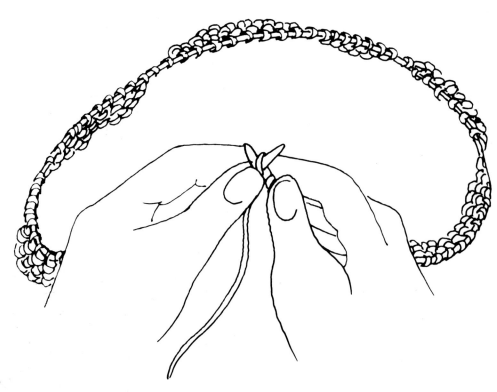

holding yarn in the left hand, you will find that it is also the speediest.

And so comes the question, straight or circular? It is a matter of preference.

Knitters who use circular needles love the light weight, the speed with which they can knit, and the seamless finish. (One Icelandic knitter who produces four or five sweaters a week can knit in the dark, working only by feel.)

Those who prefer straight needles say the weight and length of the needles give balance and keep their stitches even. Because there are seams, there is some margin for adjusting size to fit, by taking in or letting out. When the needle is long enough to tuck under one arm, this allows some freedom of movement. The right hand carries the yarn in a smooth rhythm.

Here is a summary of the advantages of circular needles:
• You never lose a needle.
• If you slide your stitches onto the cable when you are not working, they will not fall off.
• Because the needles are lightweight, they are speedy.
• The weight of the knitting is evenly distributed, not all on one side.
• You can also use circular needles to knit back and forth, as on straight needles.
• You need never change back and forth from knitting rows to purling rows to create stockinette stitch.

Sizes are not marked on circular needles. If necessary, measure the size of the needle with a needle gauge. When the needle just passes through a hole without stopping, you have found the correct size. As you knit on circular needles, mark the end of each row with a row marker so that you do not lose your place. When reading a straight-needle pattern, the basic rule is to read the wrong-side rows from the end to the beginning, exactly reversing them—switching purls to knits and knits to purls.

TO BEGIN

With a pair of needles, some yarn, and your fingers, you can create a garment that will stretch and spring back into shape, that never creases, that is designed for summer or winter, and that can be made quickly and easily expressly for you.

For all its seemingly intricate patterns and textures, knitting is basically only two simple stitches, knit and purl. Once you have practiced these two enough to work them smoothly and quickly, a whole new world will open up to you. You will soon realize that there are only four ways to do even the most complex-looking decorative knitting: with stitch textures, with color changes, with surface stitching done after you've knitted your garment, or with some combination of these three.

Today's easy-fitting sweaters make it simple to knit even intricately patterned designs because you can knit straight pieces without having to worry too much about shaping. When the same number of stitches is maintained in every row, it is much easier to work out pattern repeats.

If you have never knitted before, practice a little first. Begin by knitting a swatch of stockinette stitch so that you can develop a smooth rhythm before you begin an actual garment. Learn the basic way of forming the stitches first. Then practice holding the needles with the yarn in either the left or the right hand. This has nothing to do with being right-handed or left-handed—it is really a method of working that allows you to knit fast, by feel. In knitting, you are ambidextrous, and all of your fingers on both hands work together. (Left-handed knitters should simply hold the diagrams that follow in front of a mirror.)

Use pure wool to start: It is stretchy, clings around the needles easily, and just as easily slides from one needle to the other.

To start your swatch, knit every row until you are proficient. The pattern this makes is called *garter stitch.* Next, try one row knit, one row purl. This pattern, called *stockinette stitch,* has a smooth side and a "rough" side with loops.

You will learn from the following pages how to knit with yarn held in the right hand (American method) and how to knit with yarn held in the left hand (Continental method). Basically, the first method is best for flat knitting on straight needles, and the second is best for circular needles, though it is not limited to them. When you knit with color changes, you will use both hands (see page 119). Once you have practiced and made some swatches, you can start with a simple pattern, such as the all-in-one sweater for a teddy bear or a child on page 34.

Patterns have a code of instructions that make them less unwieldy and easier to use. The codes are abbreviations. Rather like notes in music, they require some study before you begin. They are illustrated on page 39.

There is one last concept to master before you begin a garment—gauge. This simple but important mathematical calculation affects the fit of a sweater. Gauge is explained on page 33.

Combining color changes with textures gives you yet another dimension, and when you finally take needle in hand to add decorative stitches on top of your finished knitting, you will realize that the possibilities are unlimited.

You can try making a swatch of any of the stitch patterns shown on the following pages. Then adapt them to any of the basic shapes of sweaters in the book. Experiment with different thicknesses and kinds of yarn to find your favorites. You will be amazed at the variety of effects you can achieve with the same stitch. The textured Skye sweater on page 55 is knitted in natural, undyed sheep's wool. The striped cotton sweater in smooth stockinette stitch shown beside it seems entirely unrelated, yet it is made in the identical shape. On page 50, the same cascading waterfall stitch is shown in three different garments. These illustrate how you can change the stitch and use the same shape, or keep the stitch pattern and change the shape—with entirely different results.

Once you have followed some of the techniques shown here letter-for-letter, you will feel bold enough to try your own ideas. Use the special section at the end of this book to create unique sweaters of your own design.

CASTING ON

This method is ideal for knitting with the yarn held in the right hand. (Alternate method is shown on page 24.)

Begin by making a slip knot. Form a loop at one end of the yarn and draw another loop through it, just as if making a shoelace bow.

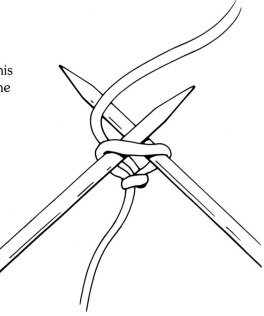

Slip the second loop onto the needle and draw the thread tight to form the first stitch.

Next, slide the right needle through this stitch from front to back and under the left needle. Wrap the working strand around the needle as shown. (The working strand is the one attached to the ball of yarn.)

Holding the working strand under
tension, draw it through the first stitch.
Pull it out to form a loop.

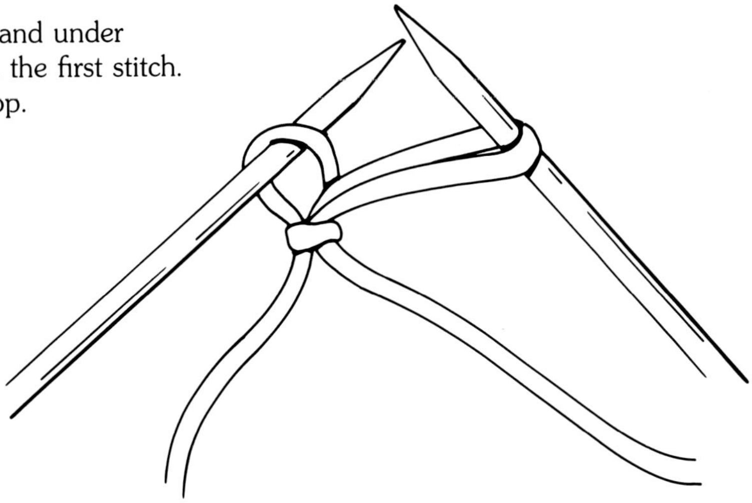

Twist the loop with the needle or with
finger and thumb of the right hand and
slip it onto the left needle.

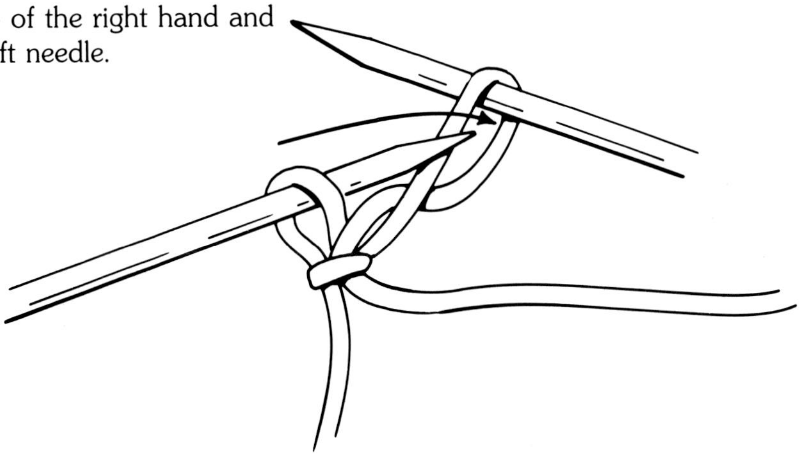

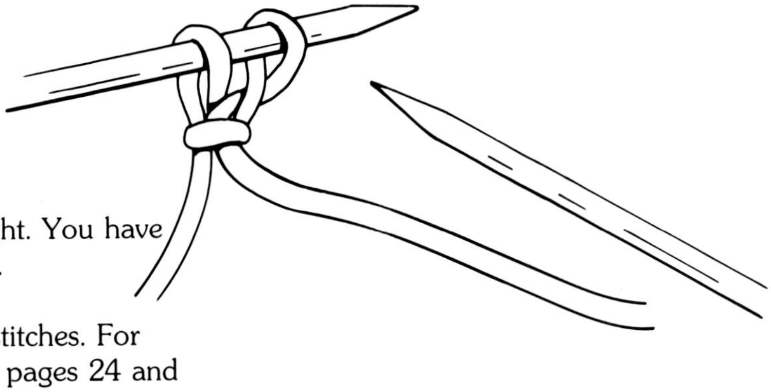

Gently draw the thread tight. You have
cast on your second stitch.

Repeat to form a row of stitches. For
other ways to cast on, see pages 24 and
25.

KNITTING: AMERICAN METHOD
(Yarn Held in Right Hand)

The right-handed method is usually the most comfortable for flat knitting (knitting on straight needles). If the needle is long enough to be supported under one arm, the right hand is free to rock the yarn like a shuttle while the left hand manipulates the left-hand needle. Practice will make these movements very smooth. You may also try resting the right-hand needle on top, cradled between the thumb and forefinger, as though holding a pencil. Speed knitting with the right needle stuck into a belt or waistband, leaves the right hand free to manipulate the yarn while the left hand manipulates the needles. This ancient method was used in the sixteenth century (see page 7) and is especially useful when the yarn is constantly being moved from back to front, as in ribbing (k1, p1).

KNIT AND PURL Begin by weaving the working thread through your fingers. Bring it through between the fourth and fifth fingers.

Take it around the little finger, over the third and fourth fingers, and behind the forefinger, as shown.

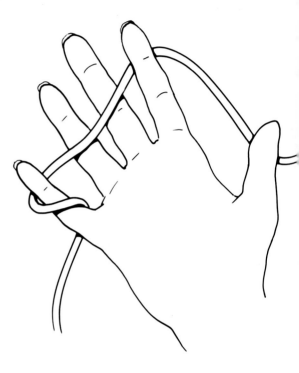

KNIT With the needle resting in your right hand, rather as if holding a pen, hold the yarn out taut with your index finger. Slide the right needle under the left, through the stitch.

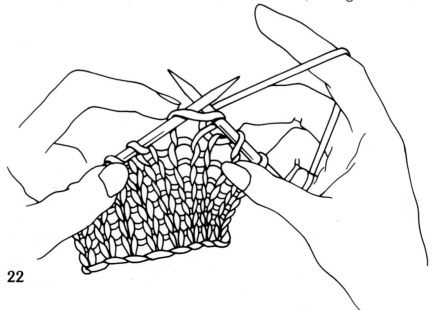

22

Move the forefinger forward, like a shuttle, to carry the yarn around the needle. The thumb rests, moving only slightly. (If long needles are being used, tuck the right needle under the arm for increased stability.)

Having wrapped the thread around the needle, ease it through the stitch, holding the right needle with thumb and forefinger, and keeping the yarn taut.

PURL With the yarn forward, slide the right needle through the front of the stitch from right to left. With the thumb at rest, carry the yarn forward with the forefinger to wrap it around the needle from right to left.

With the needle still resting on the hand and the yarn taut, rotate the needle to draw the yarn back through the stitch, forming a loop. As the stitch slides off the needle, the purl stitch is formed.

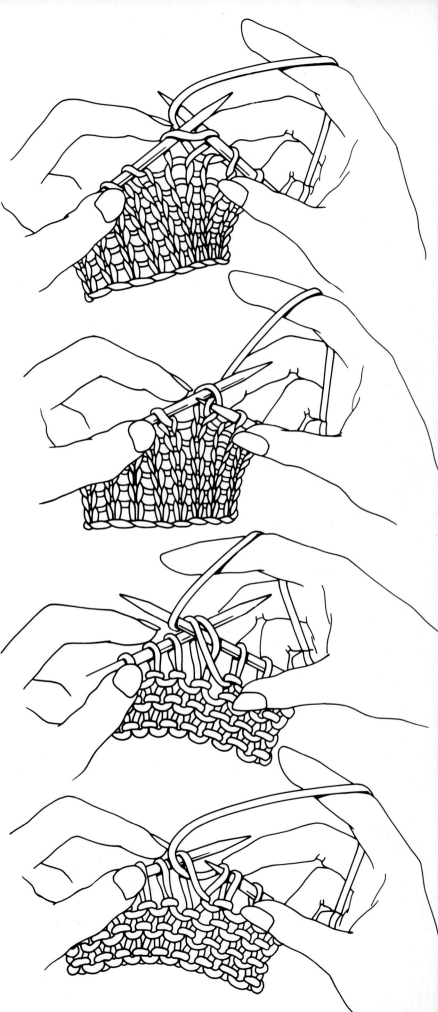

CASTING ON

This method is ideal for knitting with the yarn held in the left hand. Choose the method you prefer (see page 20).

This is a quick and easy cast-on method ideal for short or circular needles. Use two needles and draw one out afterward, because the stitches tend to tighten.

Double over a length of yarn from the ball, approximately three times as long as you think the width of the cast-on stitches will be. (The extra length is useful for seaming afterward.)

Make a loop. Slide it over the needles and let the ends dangle, holding them under your little finger, as shown.

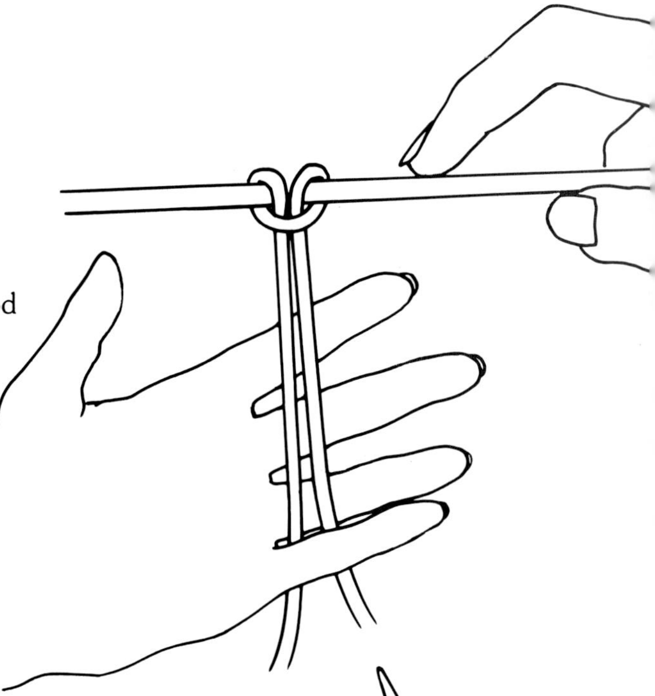

Slide forefinger and thumb through between the strands.

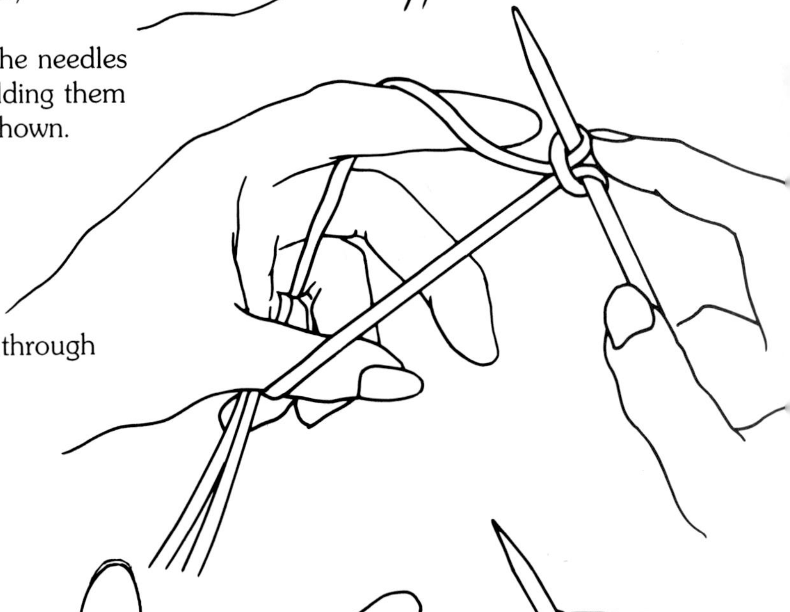

Bring thumb back, as shown.

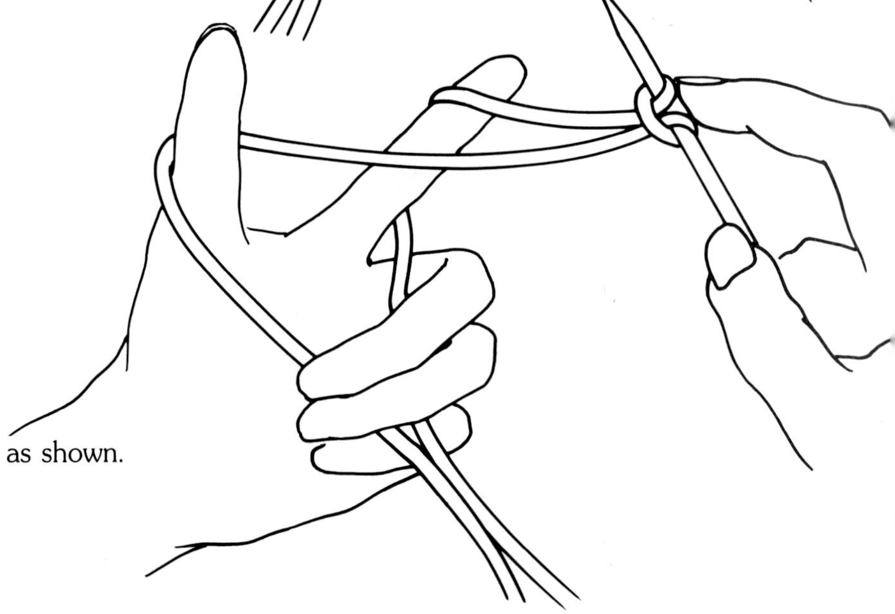

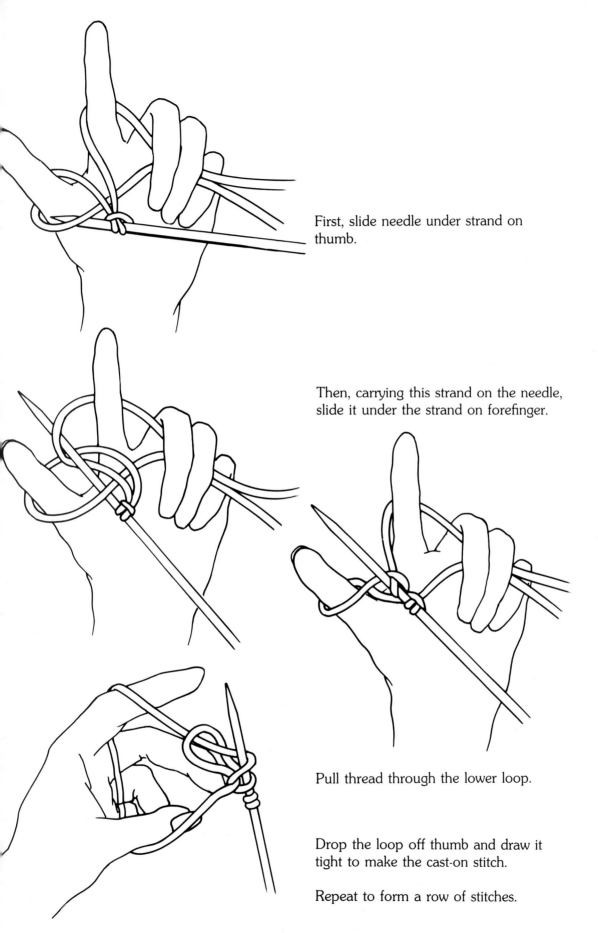

First, slide needle under strand on thumb.

Then, carrying this strand on the needle, slide it under the strand on forefinger.

Pull thread through the lower loop.

Drop the loop off thumb and draw it tight to make the cast-on stitch.

Repeat to form a row of stitches.

KNITTING: CONTINENTAL METHOD
(Yarn Held in Left Hand)

KNIT AND PURL For short or round needles, this method is the speediest, as the weight is held equally in both hands and both hands move together.

Hook the little finger of your left hand over the yarn.

Then wind the yarn over your third, under your fourth, and over your forefinger, as shown.

KNIT To form a knit stitch, hold the yarn in the left hand taut. Slide the right needle from left to right through the front of the stitch on the left needle to pick up the yarn.

Still using the forefinger to hold the yarn taut, begin to wrap it around the right needle, as shown.

At the same time, rotate the right needle to hook the yarn and bring it through. Moving the thread and needle simultaneously develops the rhythm.

PURL Insert the right-hand needle in front of the left-hand needle into the stitch on the left-hand needle. Wrap the yarn around the needle as if to make a purl stitch (see page 23). While holding the yarn taut in the left hand, rotate the right needle so it swings over, picks up the yarn, and slides under the left needle to form the stitch.

Draw the purl stitch gently through. Synchronize the movements of both hands. With practice, a rhythm will develop, so that the stitches will slide off the needle without any effort.

PATTERN STITCHES

GARTER STITCH Every row is knitted. This results in ridged loops on both sides.

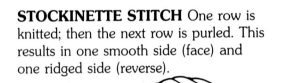

STOCKINETTE STITCH One row is knitted; then the next row is purled. This results in one smooth side (face) and one ridged side (reverse).

Right Side

Reverse Side

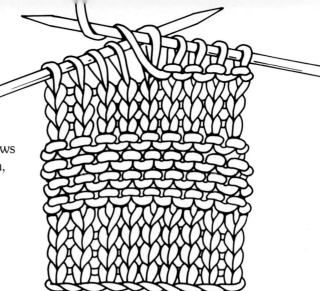

REVERSE STOCKINETTE
STITCH Two or more alternating rows of knit and purl form a raised pattern, as shown.

SEED STITCH In ribbing, each knit stitch is directly above a knit stitch in the previous row, and each purl stitch is above a purl stitch in the previous row. In seed stitch, the knits are placed above the purls and the purls above the knits. This makes a brick pattern that gives an entirely different effect from ribbing, yet the two are basically the same stitch.

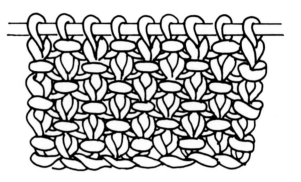

RIBBING Purl and knit stitches (or groups of stitches) alternate. Knit, bring the yarn forward, purl, and bring the yarn back. This forms a stretchy fabric. Ribbing is often used to make a band for the bottoms and cuffs of sweaters.

INCREASING

There are several ways of adding extra stitches as you work across a row, thereby widening the piece you are knitting. Some are invisible; some leave horizontal bars; some make your stitches slant to the left or to the right; and some leave openings or holes in the knitting.

Four basic methods are shown here. You will discover different techniques farther on in this book.

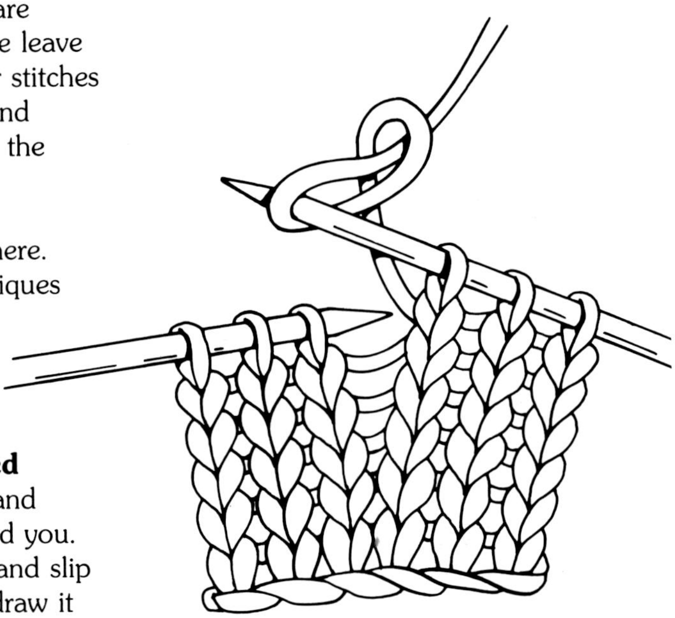

Increase by making a twisted loop: Take the working strand and make a loop with the end toward you. Twist the loop over once again and slip it over the right needle. Gently draw it tight. Result: one extra stitch formed. This method will leave a hole that will show only as the next row is knitted.

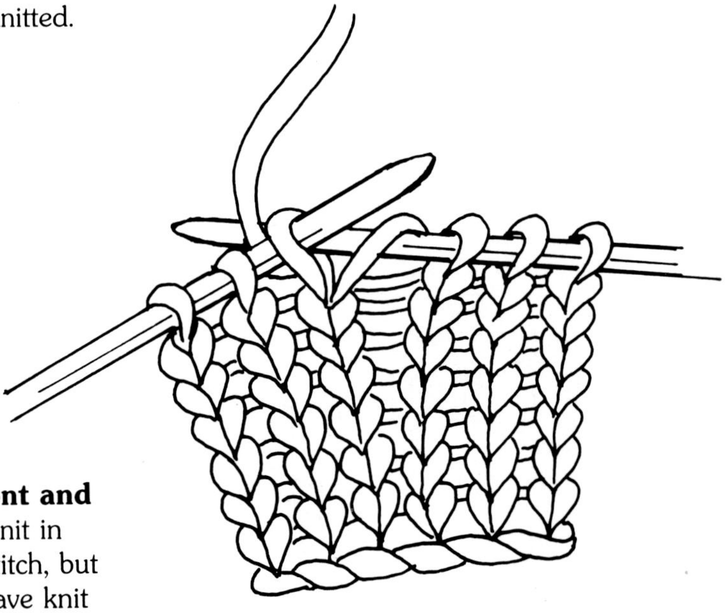

Increase by knitting in front and back of the same stitch: Knit in front as for an ordinary knit stitch, but before sliding the stitch you have knit into off the needle, knit in back of the same stitch. Result: two stitches on the needle and a small bar formed between the stitches.

Increase by picking up the stitch below the next stitch to be knitted (lifted increase): This invisible increase is extremely neat. With the right needle, pick up the stitch (purlwise) immediately below the next one to be knitted. Slide it onto the left needle. Separate the two stitches with your thumbnail and knit first into the back of the picked-up stitch and then into the back of the next stitch to be knitted. Result: two stitches.

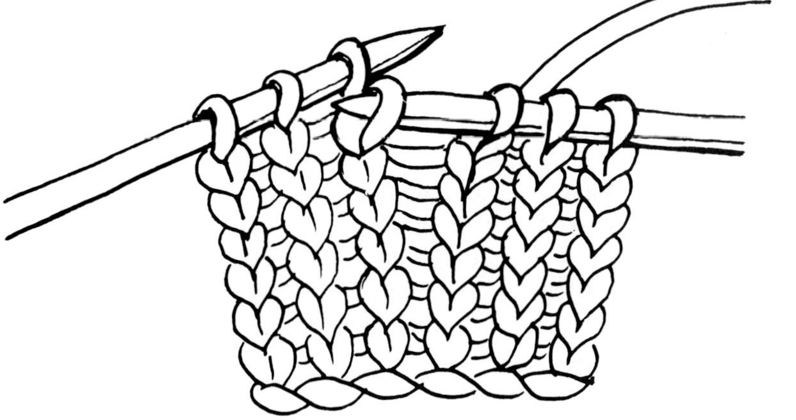

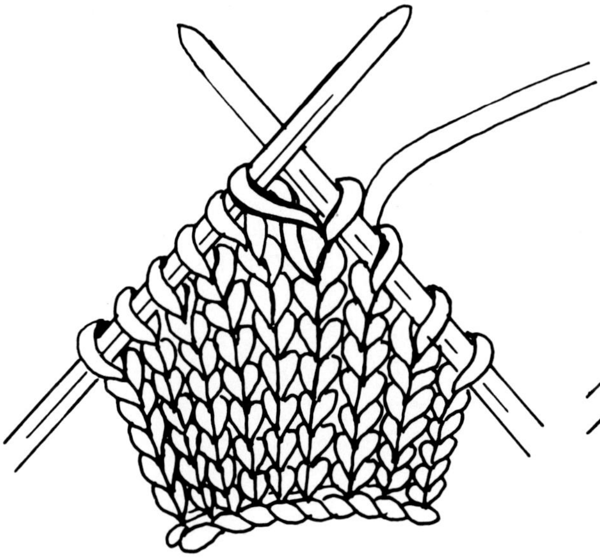

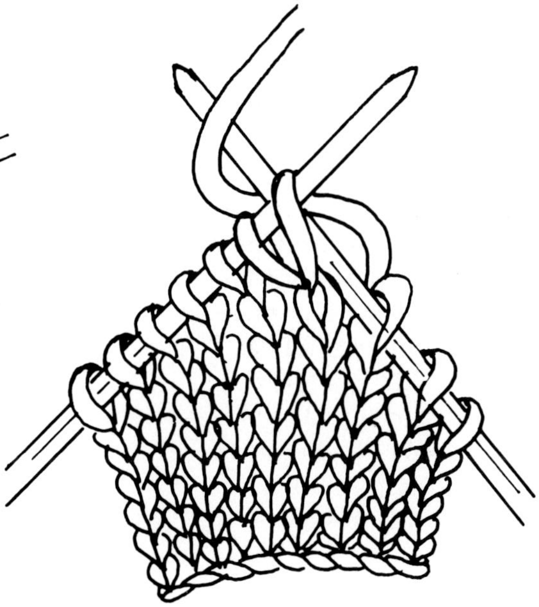

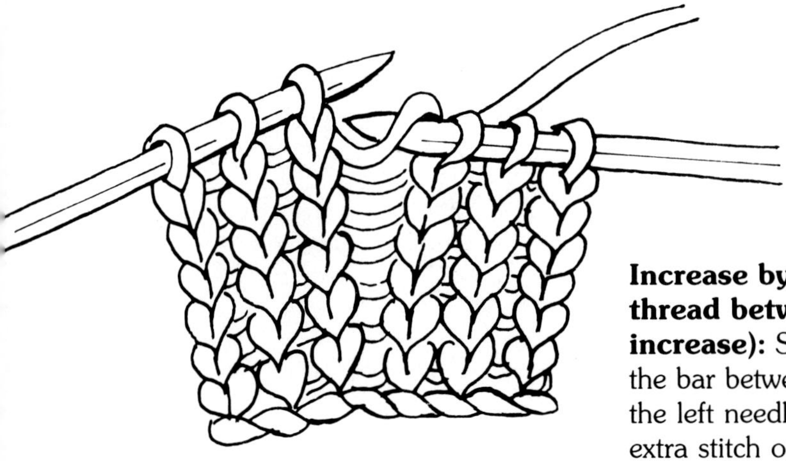

Increase by picking up the running thread between stitches (raised increase): Slide the right needle under the bar between the stitches. Lift it onto the left needle and knit it. Result: one extra stitch on the needle.

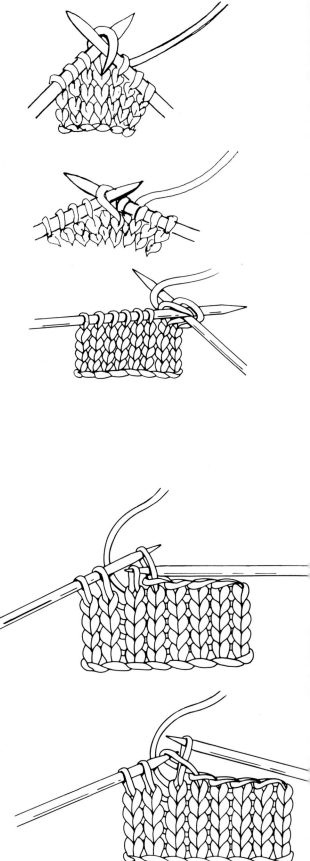

DECREASING

Knit two stitches together and they become one. Result: one stitch fewer on the needle.

SLIP STITCH: Always slip one stitch from the needle purlwise—as if to purl—unless the instructions say otherwise. Take the stitch over from one needle to the other without knitting or purling it.

PSSO first alternate: Slip the first stitch. Knit the next stitch, and then pass the slipped stitch over the knitted stitch, as shown.

PSSO second alternate: Instead of using PSSO to decrease, you can use an alternate method that gives a neater finish. Slip two stitches *knitwise*—as if to knit—one at a time. Then insert the left needle through the two stitches from left to right, above the right needle. Wrap the yarn around the right needle and knit the two stitches together.

BINDING OFF

Bind or cast off a row of stitches as follows:

Knit the first two stitches. Then lift the first stitch over the second stitch, as shown.

Drop the loop off the left needle. Knit the next stitch and repeat the process, lifting the second stitch over the third stitch. This results in a smooth, chained band along the bound-off edge.

To bind off in purl stitch, repeat the procedure, but make purl instead of knit stitches as you move across the row.

If two sweaters are knitted to exactly the same pattern, one using fine wool with fine needles and the other using bulky yarn with jumbo needles, the contrast in size will be as great or greater than that shown here. This illustrates how a small difference over a 1-inch (2.5-centimeter) area can multiply into a huge difference over a whole sweater.

GAUGE

Any knitter knows that nothing is more disappointing than seeing the hard work of a project wasted because the finished product is too big or too small. This can be avoided by establishing your gauge right at the beginning. Gauge is the number of stitches and rows per inch (or centimeter) in your sweater. Your tension—how tightly or loosely you knit—as well as the weight and thickness of your yarn and the size of your needles, controls the gauge and therefore the finished size of the knitting.

Every pattern gives the gauge to achieve the correct finished measurements right at the beginning. With the yarn you will be using and the needle size you have selected, make a swatch at least 4 inches (10 centimeters) square. Lay it flat, being careful not to stretch it. Place a plastic ruler or tape measure on top of it, marking a 2-inch (5-centimeter) square with straight pins. Measure in the center, because the edges are apt to be

distorted. Count the number of stitches and the number of rows within the pins to see if your actual knitting measures up to the gauge specifications on the pattern. If your gauge is off, knit another swatch using a different needle size. A smaller needle will increase your gauge, giving you more stitches per inch. A larger needle will give you fewer stitches per inch. Remember, of course, since you've measured a 2-inch (5-centimeter) section, to divide by 2 to give you the number of stitches per inch. No matter how impatient you are to start your actual knitting, it is always worthwhile to check your gauge first. If you are off even by half a stitch, it will change the size of your sweater or project.

A sample swatch is equally important if you are designing your own pattern. It allows you to determine the number of stitches to cast on and the number of rows to work. Always make the swatch in the same pattern stitch as the main body of your sweater. Continue to check the gauge as your work progresses.

ALL-IN-ONE SWEATER

A simple way to learn knitting after you have knitted a practice swatch of ribbing and stockinette stitch is to make a small all-in-one sweater for a teddy bear or a child. Because the sweater is knitted all in one piece, it is quick and easy. As you gain experience, you can vary textures and color combinations. You can even vary the size of the sweater, making small all-in-one sweaters as decorative pins or Christmas ornaments, or large all-in-one sweaters for adults.

FOR A TEDDY BEAR

Instructions are given for a very small bear, measuring 8 inches (20 centimeters) around and 2½ inches (6.25 centimeters) from shoulder to waist. For larger bears, simply increase the number of stitches cast on, holding the knitting up to the bear's tummy to measure the number of extra stitches needed. Be sure to allow a few extra for the rounding of the tummy! Increase all the other measurements proportionately.

See page 39 for an explanation of any abbreviations you are unsure of.

MATERIALS:

Yarn: One 1¾-ounce (50-gram) ball of knitting sport weight

Needles: Straight knitting needles, U.S. size 3 (Continental size 3¼) Double-pointed needles, set of 2 *Or sizes needed to obtain gauge*

GAUGE: In stockinette stitch: 13 stitches = 2 inches (5 centimeters)

The sweater is worked all in one piece, starting from the lower back.
Cast on 26 sts with straight needles.
ROWS 1-4: Work even in k1, p1 ribbing.

ROWS 5-12: Work even in St st (k 1 row, p 1 row).

ROW 13: Cast on 6 sts at beginning of row; k32.

ROW 14: Cast on 6 sts at beginning of row; then k2, p34, k2.

ROW 15: K38.

ROW 16: K2, p34, k2.

ROWS 17-30: Repeat Rows 15 and 16.

ROW 31: K10, bind off 18, k10.

ROW 32: K2, p8, cast on 18, p8, k2.

ROWS 33-48: Repeat Rows 15 and 16.

ROW 49: Bind off 6 sts; k across.

ROW 50: Bind off 6 sts; k across.

ROWS 51-58: Work even in St st.

ROWS 59-62: Work even in k1, p1 ribbing.
Bind off.

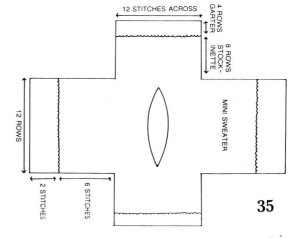

12 STITCHES ACROSS

4 ROWS GARTER

8 ROWS STOCK-INETTE

12 ROWS

MINI SWEATER

2 STITCHES

6 STITCHES

35

FOR A CHILD

SIZES: 2 [4, 6]

MATERIALS:

Yarn: Two 4-ounce (100-gram) balls (1 white, 1 blue) of knitting worsted weight

Needles: Straight knitting needles, U.S. sizes 5 and 7 (Continental sizes 4 and 5)

Double-pointed needles, U.S. size 5

Or sizes needed to obtain gauge

GAUGE: With larger needles, in stockinette stitch: 9 stitches = 2 inches (5 centimeters)

STRIPE PATTERN: 2 rows white, 2 rows blue

The sweater is worked all in one piece, starting from the lower back.

With smaller needles, cast on 52 [56, 60] sts.

Work in k1, p1 ribbing for 1½ inches (3.75 centimeters): about 7 rows.

Change to larger needles. Work even in St st and stripe pattern until piece measures 9 inches (23 centimeters) [10 inches (25.5 centimeters), 11 inches (28 centimeters)] overall.

Cast on 8 sts at end of next 2 rows.

Continue in stripe pattern until work measures 4 inches (10 centimeters) [4½ inches (11.5 centimeters), 5 inches (12.5 centimeters)] from cast-on sts.

Form neck opening: Bind off center 26 [28, 30] sts. Join a second ball of yarn and work each side separately for 1 inch (2.5 centimeters).

Next row: Rejoin work. K21 [22, 23] sts; cast on 26 [28, 30] sts for center neck, k21 [22, 23] sts. Work even in pattern for 4 inches (10 centimeters)

[4½ inches (11.5 centimeters), 5 inches (12.5 centimeters)].

Bind off 8 sts beginning next 2 rows.

Continue to work in pattern for 9 inches (23 centimeters) [10 inches (25.5 centimeters), 11 inches (28 centimeters)] more.

Change back to smaller needles. Work k1, p1 ribbing for 1½ inches (3.75 centimeters): about 7 rows. Bind off in ribbing.

Neck opening: First, refer to page 172 for information on picking up sts on a bound-off edge. Then, with double-pointed needles, pick up 56 [60, 64] sts and work k1, p1 ribbing for 3 inches (7.5 centimeters). Bind off loosely in ribbing. Sew side seams.

BEAR'S HAT

Knit this hat in narrow stripes of contrasting colors, using fluffy mohair. Because it is neater without a seam, use double-pointed needles.

MATERIALS:

Yarn: 1 ball *each* of 2 contrasting colors of mohair or knitting worsted weight

Needles: Set of 4 double-pointed needles, U.S. size 7 (Continental size 5)

Or size needed to obtain gauge

Notions: Tapestry needle, lightweight cardboard

GAUGE: In stockinette stitch: with mohair, 11 stitches = 2 inches (5 centimeters); with worsted weight, 9 stitches = 2 inches (5 centimeters)

When changing colors horizontally, the first right-side row must always be knitted to make a clean line. On a purl row, the contrasting color will make a thin stripe of loops.

Cast on 72 sts. Divide to place 24 sts on each of 3 needles. K with the 4th needle.

ROWS 1-5: K1, p1 ribbing.
ROW 6: With color A, knit. Beg striped band of St st:
ROW 7: With color A, purl.
ROW 8: With color B, knit.
ROW 9: With color B, purl.
Repeat Rows 6 through 9 until a tube of 15 rows of alternating stripes has been formed.
For the last row, *k 2 tog. Repeat from * all around. End off by sewing through each st with a tapestry needle. Draw up tight and secure the end.

Make pompon: Cut 2 cardboard disks (shirt cardboard is fine) a little wider than the desired width of the pompon. Make identical holes in the center of the disks. Roll lengths of yarn small enough to fit through the center holes. Place the disks together and wrap with wool until there is enough wrapping to close the center holes. Slip the point of your scissors between the disks and clip the wool all around the outer edge. Draw a strand of yarn between the disks and wrap it around several times. Secure it with a double knot. Leave the ends long for attaching the pompon to the hat. Slip the disks off and fluff the pompon out.

BEAR'S SCARF

You can knit a striped scarf for a bear in stockinette stitch with a long fringe at either end to match the hat and sweater. The long, narrow strip tends to curl along both side edges, however. You might take advantage of this by stitching the curled edges together and making the seam the center back of the scarf. Perhaps a more interesting solution is double-knitting—a simple technique of slipping 1 and knitting 1 alternately. This results in two separated sides of knitting, like a flat tube joined only at top and bottom. It can be done either in stockinette stitch or in garter stitch. The two sides of the scarf will be identical.

MATERIALS:

Yarn: 1 ball *each* of 2 contrasting colors of mohair or knitting worsted weight
Needles: Straight knitting needles, U.S. size 8 (Continental size 5½)
Or size needed to obtain gauge

GAUGE: In stockinette stitch: with mohair, 11 stitches = 2 inches (5 centimeters); with worsted weight, 9 stitches = 2 inches (5 centimeters)

To Make a Striped Scarf in Plain Stockinette Stitch: With color A, cast on 22 sts.
ROWS 1, 2, 5, 6, 9, 10: With color A, knit.
ROWS 3, 4, 7, 8, 11, 12: With color B, purl.
Repeat, alternating colors and twisting yarn at the edge to carry the color up to the next band (see page 116), until the scarf is the desired length.
Make a loop fringe at each end, using colors A and B together.

To Make a Scarf in Double Stockinette Stitch: With color A, cast on 44 sts. (Your scarf will be 22 sts wide.)
ROW 1: With color A, *p1, sl1. Repeat to end of row. Always cast on an even number of sts when you do double-knitting, so you will always end the row with a p1 and begin with a sl1. Always sl the sts as if to p. Sl the first st, bring the yarn forward, p the next st, take the yarn to the back, sl

the next st, and repeat across the row. Continue until the scarf is the desired length. Bind off all sts.

To Make a Scarf in Garter
Stitch: Simply k instead of p. Sl the sts purlwise, but do not carry the yarn backward and forward.

Once you have discovered the joys of double-knitting on 2 needles, you may decide to make leggings, socks, or mittens for bears (or people!). To leave the ends open, cast on half the stitches on one double-pointed needle, and, without breaking the yarn, cast on the other half on another double-pointed needle. With a third double-pointed needle, alternately sl1 and k1 from each needle until all are on one needle. Continue knitting with 2 needles until the end. Then pick up every other stitch onto a second needle. Cast off each side separately and add fringe.

CROCHET STITCHES

Crochet: Crocheting is a series of loops created on a single hooked needle. It is extremely useful in knitting for decorative edging, buttonholes, collars, cuffs, and creative embellishments.

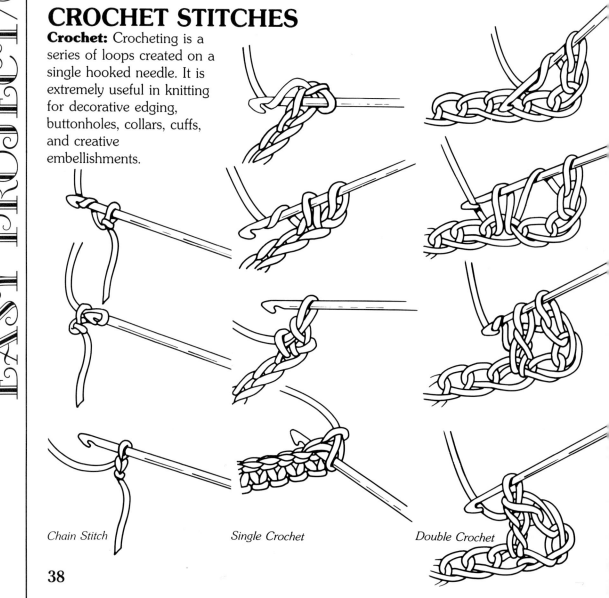

Chain Stitch   *Single Crochet*   *Double Crochet*

ABBREVIATIONS

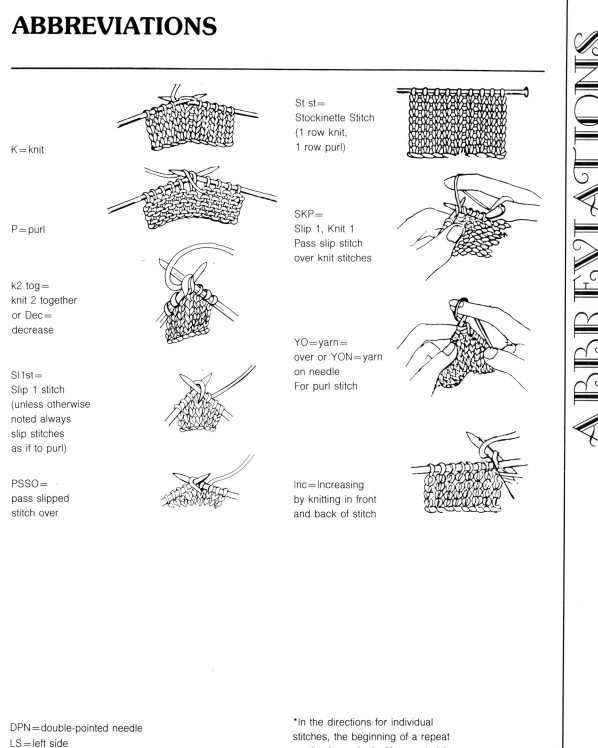

K = knit

P = purl

k2 tog =
knit 2 together
or Dec =
decrease

Sl1st =
Slip 1 stitch
(unless otherwise
noted always
slip stitches
as if to purl)

PSSO =
pass slipped
stitch over

St st =
Stockinette Stitch
(1 row knit,
1 row purl)

SKP =
Slip 1, Knit 1
Pass slip stitch
over knit stitches

YO = yarn =
over or YON = yarn
on needle
For purl stitch

Inc = Increasing
by knitting in front
and back of stitch

DPN = double-pointed needle
LS = left side
RS = right side
WS = wrong side
sc = single crochet
dc = double crochet

*In the directions for individual
stitches, the beginning of a repeat
section is marked with an asterisk
(*). The instructions that come after
the asterisk are to be repeated as
many times as specified, or else to
the end of the row.

Child's Snakes and
Ladders
Cardigan (page 163)

Child's "Find the Letter"
Sweater
(page 154)

So that you can learn basic techniques and apply them to any sweater, not just the ones shown here, this book is divided into four sections.

The first section, "Texture," shows how a sweater in one color can have drama—because of raised patterns, openwork lace, or three-dimensional sculptural effects.

Color changing, called *intarsia,* can turn your sweater into a work of art, with all the verve of an impressionist painting. Or it can be used to make overall repeat patterns like a jacquard fabric, creating kaleidoscopes of color.

Child's Humpty-Dumpty Sweater (page 166)

Nantucket Sweater
(page 138)

**Sheep and
Hearts Sweater
(page 127)**

**Bobbles and
Bands Jacket (page 114)
Contemporary Fair Isle Pullover (page 121)**

Autumn Leaves Sweater (page 150)

Lacy Cable Pullover (page ...)

Silk Honeycomb Pullover (page 102)

Tyrolean
Embroidered
Jacket
(page 144)

Left to right:
**Cascading
Waterfall
Sweater and
Camisole
(pages 96 and 97)**

**Pink Cloud
Sweater
(page 92)**

Left to right:
Dazzling Diamond Weave Sweaters (page 108)

White Cloud Evening Sweater (page 110)

Skye Blue
Sweater and
Skye Sampler Sweater
(pages 66 and 67)

Soft Cable
Sweater
(page 60)

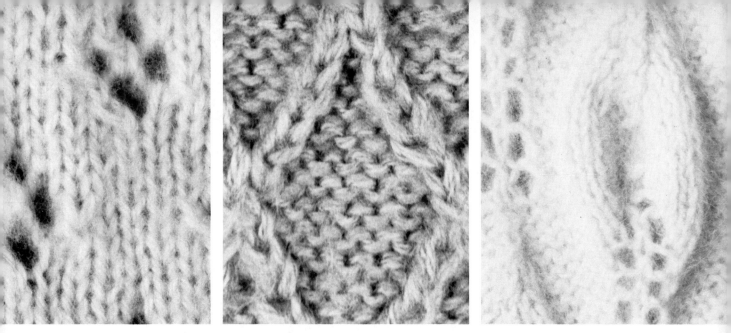

TEXTURE

The textured patterns that follow are just to get you started. You can make practice swatches in different yarns—and then perhaps choose to make the sweater that follows each pattern in the yarn suggested. This will give you a feeling for the basic shape and style of the sweater in relation to the scale of the stitch pattern, its texture, and the kind of yarn.

There are certain things always to keep in mind about the sweater patterns. When counting rows to establish the length of the garment, remember that the cast-on stitches do not count as a row. The first row is the row knitted into the cast-on stitches. When measuring, always measure the piece from the bottom to the top of your needles.

Each stitch pattern is given with the number of stitches you need for each repeat. For instance, for simple knit 1, purl 1 ribbing, the number cast on must be a multiple of 2 so that you are certain to begin each row with a knit stitch and end it with a purl. If you were to work the same knit 1, purl 1 ribbing on an odd number of stitches, your row would end with a knit stitch, and your next row would begin with a knit stitch. This would result in seed stitch instead of ribbing (see page 29).

For the same reason, when you are working certain patterns with straight needles, you may have to add stitches to the multiples you cast on in order to bring the pattern out symmetrically on either side.

Many knitters like to add a stitch on either side for selvedge, to make a firm seam on each edge. This is essential when the last stitch of a pattern requires a yarn-over (yo) instead of a knitted stitch. To make the selvedge smooth, slip the first stitch of every row and work the last stitch in pattern. To use this method, remember to add 2 stitches to the number required by the pattern when you cast on.

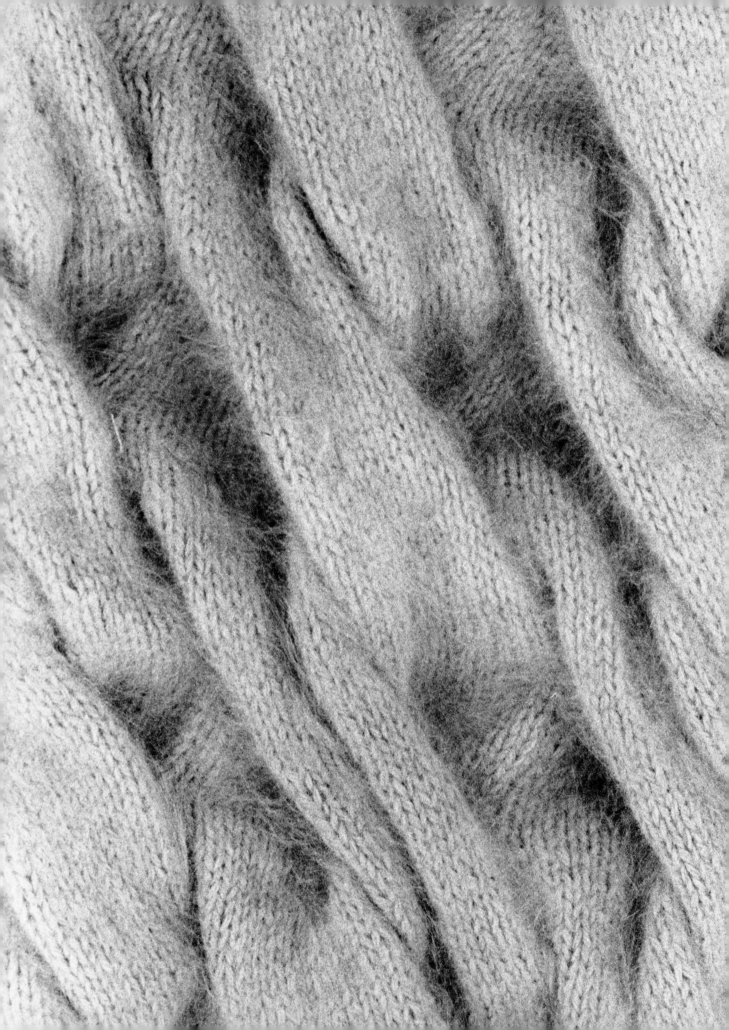

HOW TO MAKE A SOFT CABLE

Cables are formed by switching one group of stitches with another, knitting them out of sequence. This forms a raised rope, which gives the stitch its name. Cables can be either wide or narrow, with completely different results. The soft cable is a new twist on this classic theme. It has such an entirely different look that no one would guess it is worked in basically the same way. The pattern is done in sections, by knitting separate strips on one needle. When the strips are long enough to be twisted, the alternating strips are put onto a holder and then knitted back onto the needle in reverse order to form the cable. The one thing that makes the soft cable unique is the width of each band. These are so wide that each individual strip must be knitted with its own separate ball of yarn. To avoid tangles, you may prefer to wind sufficient yarn for each cable onto its own bobbin before beginning.

This pattern is worked on multiples of 40 sts plus 20 sts.

ROWS 1 AND 3: Knit.

ROWS 2 AND 4: Purl.

ROW 5: K10; leave yarn hanging; *working with new yarn, k20; leave yarn hanging; repeat from * until there are 10 sts left in the row; leave yarn hanging; working with a new ball of yarn, k10.

ROW 6 (AND ALL ALTERNATE ROWS): Purl.

ROWS 7-23 (ODD-NUMBERED ROWS ONLY): Repeat Row 5.

ROW 25 (CROSS-CABLE ROW): K10, leave yarn hanging; *working with new yarn, k 1st set of 20 sts onto DPN; leave needle in front of work; k20 (2nd set of sts); k 20 sts from DPN (1st cable

twist made); repeat from * until 10 sts remain in row; leave yarn hanging; working with new yarn, k10.

ROWS 27 AND 29: Knit.

Repeat from Row 1 for pattern.

Because of the width and length of the cables, large openings are formed between each one. When the whole piece is finished, these gaps can easily be closed by seaming the edges together on the wrong side, using a tapestry needle and matching yarn (see page 172).

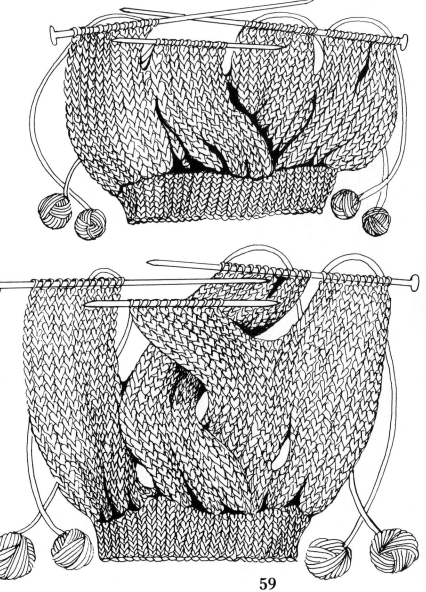

59

SOFT CABLE SWEATER
(Color photo page 56)

Soft as a cloud, this sculptured-looking sweater is beautiful in angora. Fine mohair gives the same misty effect, with lighter weight. In soft cotton, the cables appear more defined. Whether you use textured or soft yarn, the effect is unique.

SIZE: Medium

MATERIALS:
Yarn: Twenty-six 36-yard (33-meter) balls of 100% pure angora
or
Eight 230-yard (210-meter) balls of 60% acrylic, 40% mohair
Needles: 17-inch-long straight knitting needles, U.S. sizes 5 and 7 (Continental sizes 4 and 5)
Or sizes needed to obtain gauge
Notions: 10 bobbins, double-pointed needles

GAUGE: With larger needles, in stockinette stitch, 5 stitches and 6 rows = 1 inch (2.5 centimeters)

60

FINISHED MEASUREMENTS:
Bust: 36 inches (92 centimeters)
Sleeve (measured at underarm seam): 21 inches (53.5 centimeters)
Length: 22 inches (56 centimeters)

BACK
With smaller needles, cast on 90 sts and work in k1, p1 ribbing for 3 inches (7.5 centimeters). Change to larger needles and St st.
ROW 1 (INC ROW): Inc in every st by knitting in front and in back of each (180 sts).
ROWS 2 AND 4: Purl.
ROW 3: Knit.
ROW 5 (RS): *Beg soft cable pattern:* Wind yarn on 10 bobbins. K10; leave yarn hanging; *working with new yarn, k20; leave yarn hanging; repeat from * until 10 sts remain in row; with new yarn, k10. Result: 8 separate sets of 20 sts on the needle, plus 1 set of 10 sts at either end.
ROW 6: Repeat Row 5, but p instead of k.
ROWS 7-12: Alternate Rows 5 and 6 (3 repeats in all).
ROW 13 (CROSS-CABLE ROW): K10; leave yarn hanging; *working with new yarn, k 1st set of 20 sts onto DPN; leave in front of work; k 20 sts (2nd set); k 20 sts from DPN (1st cable twist made);

repeat from * until 10 sts remain in row; working with new yarn, k10. You will have 4 complete cable twists plus a band of 10 sts at each side.

ROWS 14–22 (EVEN-NUMBERED ROWS ONLY): P all 180 sts without joining.

ROWS 15–21 (ODD-NUMBERED ROWS ONLY): K all 180 sts without joining.

ROW 23 AND FOLLOWING: Repeat Rows 5–21 to make 5 cable twists, each cable approximately 6 inches (15.25 centimeters) long, on each of the 4 cable sections. Back will measure approximately 22 inches (56 centimeters) overall. Bind off loosely. On WS, sew up openings.

FRONT

Work same as for back.

SLEEVE

With smaller needles, cast on 46 sts and work k1, p1 ribbing for 2½ inches (6.25 centimeters). *Change to larger needles and St st:*

ROW 1: Inc in every st as before (92 sts).

ROWS 2 AND 4: Purl.

ROW 3: Knit.

ROW 5 (RS): K26; leave yarn hanging; with new yarn, k20; leave yarn hanging; with new yarn, k20; leave yarn hanging; with new yarn, k26; leave yarn hanging. Continue in pattern to make 3 complete cables (4 cable twists) up center of sleeve. *At the same time,* inc 1 st, each side, at end of every inch until cables are complete, ending with Row 23 of pattern.

Bind off 26 sts. Put side-panel sts, each set of 20 sts, and other side-panel sts on DPN and bind off remaining 26 sts.

Follow pattern to Row 23 to make one complete twist, working inc sts in St st.

Bind off loosely.

Work another sleeve in the same manner.

COLLAR

With larger needles, cast on 2 separate sets of 20 sts each. K each separately in St st for 26 inches (66 centimeters). Bind off. Twist strips together 6 times. Sew ends to form circle.

FINISHING

Sew side seams. Sew underarm seams and set in sleeves with 1 twist of cable continuing across shoulder. Join front and back to this cable twist at shoulders. Attach collar.

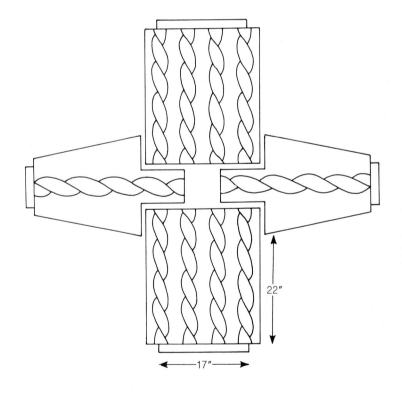

HOW TO MAKE SKYE STITCHES

Natural, homespun yarn that has not been bleached to remove the lanolin is a wonderful fiber to show off these patterns. The firm texture will delineate your stitch patterns beautifully. You can collect swatches of these and other patterns and arrange them in horizontal bands between rows of garter stitch or reverse stockinette stitch, as shown in the sweater on page 65.

Most cables are formed by holding a group of stitches on a separate needle to the back or front of the knitting and then knitting them back onto the needle out of sequence to form a twist. Mock cable is formed simply by knitting the stitches out of sequence as you move down the row. This pattern is made on every fourth row of knit 2, purl 2 ribbing. You knit into the second stitch of the rib first, and, without dropping it off the needle, knit into the first stitch, and then drop the two stitches off the needle at the same time. This simple pattern offers a nice variation on the ribbing used at neck, hem, and cuffs of a sweater.

MOCK CABLE RIBBING

This pattern is worked on a multiple of 2 sts, plus 2 sts for selvedge (see page 57).

ROW 1: *P2, k2; repeat from * across row, ending p2.

ROW 2: *K2, p2; repeat from * across row, ending k2.

ROW 3: *P2, k into 2nd stitch on left needle and leave on needle, k into 1st stitch on needle, drop 2 sts off left needle; repeat from * across row, ending p2.

ROW 4: Repeat Row 2.

Repeat these 4 rows for pattern.

The simplest ribbing is made by knitting 1 and purling 1 alternately across a row (see page 29). Each succeeding row follows the preceding one exactly, so vertical bars of knit and purl stitches are formed. The seed stitch is done simply by knitting the purl stitches and purling the knit stitches of the previous row. This breaks the vertical stripe pattern and gives a bricked effect. If you do this on a two-row sequence (two rows as for ribbing, next row as for seed stitch, next row following the previous row as if for ribbing, switching back to the original pattern on the fifth and sixth rows, and so on), a strong diagonal line develops, called double seed or Irish moss.

IRISH MOSS STITCH

This pattern is worked on a multiple of 2 sts, plus 2 sts for selvedge (see page 57).

ROW 1: *K1, p1; repeat from * across row, ending p1.

ROWS 2 AND 4: K the p sts and p the k sts of previous row.

ROW 3: *P1, k1; repeat from * across row, ending k1.

Repeat these 4 rows for pattern.

The diamond overlay is done by wrapping the yarn around the needle and, in subsequent rows, dropping off and slipping these "yarn-overs" to carry them up several rows without knitting them. Finally, they can be knitted back onto the needle out of sequence. These slanting lines form the diamond pattern.

DIAMOND OVERLAY

This pattern is worked on a multiple of 6 sts, plus 2 sts for selvedge (see page 57).

NOTE: Sl all sts as to p. On

even-numbered rows, sl all sts with yarn in back; on odd-numbered rows, sl all sts with yarn in front.

ROW 1 (WS): P1, *yo, p5, yo, p1; repeat from * across row, ending yo, p2.

ROW 2: K1, *sl1, drop yo off needle, k4, sl1, drop yo; repeat from * across row, ending k1.

ROWS 3 AND 5: P1, sl1, *p4, sl2; repeat from * across row, ending sl1, p1.

ROW 4: K1, sl1, *k4, sl2; repeat from * across row, ending sl1, k1.

ROW 6: K1; *drop next st to front of work, k2, pick up dropped st and k it, sl2, drop next st to front of work, sl same 2 sl sts back to left needle, pick up dropped st and k it, k2; repeat from * across row, ending k3.

ROW 7: P3; *yo, p1, yo, p5; repeat from * across, ending yo, p4.

ROW 8: K3; *(sl1, drop yo) twice, k4; repeat from * across row, ending k3.

ROWS 9 AND 11: P3; *sl2, p4; repeat from * across row, ending p3.

ROW 10: K3; *sl2, k4; repeat from * across row, ending k3.

ROW 12: K1; *sl2, drop next st to front of work, sl same 2 sl sts back onto left needle, pick up dropped st and k it; repeat from * across row, ending k1.

Repeat Rows 1–12 for pattern.

MOCK DIAMOND OVERLAY

The mock diamond overlay is done by knitting a band of stockinette stitch and then weaving the diamond on top, using a blunt tapestry needle and following a diagram. This pattern is very suitable for heavy yarn because it produces a flatter effect than the waffle pattern produced by diamond overlay. See the diagrams.

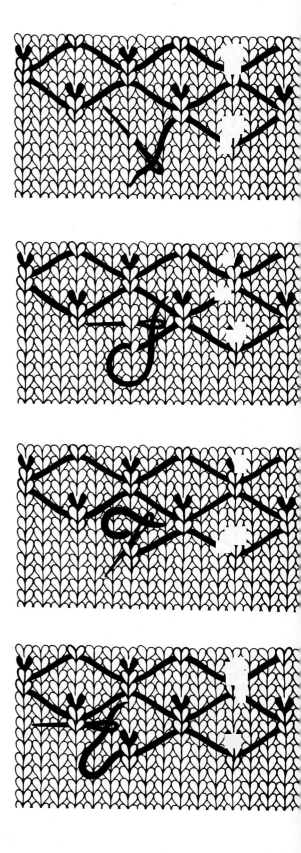

SKYE SAMPLER SWEATER

(Color photo page 55)

This traditional fisherman's sweater knit in natural homespun yarn is a sampler of textured patterns. The same-shape sweater knitted in cotton, in white and shades of blue, makes a complete contrast. These two sweaters illustrate perfectly the way you can choose any of the sweater shapes in the book and vary it with color, textured patterns, or surface embroidery.

To make the cotton sweater, see facing page.

SIZE: Extra large

MATERIALS:

Yarn: 12 balls of Fleur de Laine Pingouin natural worsted

Needles: Straight knitting needles, U.S. sizes 5 and 7 (Continental sizes 4 and 5)

Or sizes needed to obtain gauge

Notions: Double-pointed needles, tapestry needle

GAUGE: With larger needles, in stockinette stitch, 11 stitches = 2 inches (5 centimeters)

FINISHED MEASUREMENTS:

Chest: 52 inches (132 centimeters)
Sleeve (measured at underarm seam): 16½ inches (42 centimeters)
Length: 24 inches (61 centimeters)

Refer to page 63 for pattern stitches.

PATTERN A: Mock cable
PATTERN B: Irish moss (double seed)
PATTERN C: Mock diamond overlay (overlay worked after sweater is completed)

BACK

With smaller needles, cast on 118 sts and work pattern A for 3 inches (7.5 centimeters). Change to larger needles.

Band 1:

ROW 1: K, increasing 26 sts, evenly spaced, across row (144 sts).

ROW 2: Purl.

ROWS 3-6: Work garter st.

Band 2: Work pattern B for 3 inches (7.5 centimeters), ending with RS facing. Work 6 rows garter st, ending with p row.

Band 3: Work pattern C for 3 inches (7.5 centimeters), starting and ending with RS facing. Work garter st for 4 rows.

Band 4: Work pattern B for 3 inches (7.5 centimeters). Work 6 rows of garter st.

Band 5: Work pattern C for 3 inches (7.5 centimeters), ending with RS facing. Work 4 rows garter st.

Band 6: Work pattern B for 6½ inches (16.5 centimeters).

Bind off.

FRONT

Work same as for back until Band 6.

Band 6: Work pattern B for 4½ inches (11.5 centimeters).

Neck shaping: Dec for neck as follows, working pattern B: K52, bind off center 40 sts, k52. Beginning with WS facing, continue in pattern for 50 sts. K 2 tog at neck edge. Join new ball of yarn and continue each side separately. K 2 tog, k50. Continue in pattern, decreasing 1 st, every other row, each side of neck edge, twice more (49 sts each side). Work in pattern until same length as back.

Bind off both sides.

SLEEVE

With smaller needles, cast on 50 sts and work pattern A for 2½ inches (6.25 centimeters). Change to larger needles.

ROW 1 (INC ROW): K, inc 20 sts, evenly spaced, across row (70 sts).

ROW 2: Purl.

ROWS 3-6: Work garter st. Change to pattern B. Inc 1 st, each side, every 6th row, until sleeve measures 16½ inches (42 centimeters) overall.

Keeping in pattern, bind off loosely. Work another sleeve in the same manner.

COLLAR

At center front neck, with RS facing and using larger needles, pick up 29 sts to right shoulder, 48 sts across back, 29 sts from left shoulder down to center front (106 sts). Work pattern A for 2 inches (5 centimeters). Change to smaller needles. Work k2, p2 ribbing for 3½ inches (9 centimeters).

Bind off loosely in ribbing.

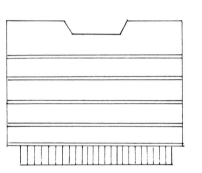 

SKYE BLUE SWEATER
(Color photo page 54)

To make the Skye blue sweater, follow the pattern and measurements for the Skye sweater, but work in sport-weight cotton yarn in stockinette stitch. In place of the pattern stitches, work bands of color. Refer to the graph for placement: Start at the bottom, working the A and B sections in deep blue, C and B in medium blue, C in pale blue, and B in white. Use white for sleeves, collar, and the half-stripes between the colors. The stripes are shown in stockinette stitch, but they would also be attractive in reverse stockinette or garter stitch.

Change colors on the face or right side of the work to keep a clean line.

HOW TO MAKE THE LATTICE PATTERN

The pattern is formed by crossing stitches on the right side of the work. You begin at the apex of the diamond. At this point, start the lattice by holding the stitch in place that you would normally knit and knit into the back of the second stitch from the needle. Then knit the first stitch and drop both stitches off the needle. The sides of the lattice are crossed either to the right or to the left, forming diagonal lines. This is done by slipping the first stitch onto a cable needle and holding it to the back of the work. Knit the next stitch, then purl the stitch from the cable needle. This crosses the stitch to the right. To cross the stitch to the left, simply hold the cable needle to the front of the work, purl the next stitch, and knit the stitch from the cable needle.

Special Abbreviations

C1R (CROSS 1 RIGHT): Sl 1 st onto cable needle and hold at back of work; k1; p1 from cable needle.

C1L (CROSS 1 LEFT): Sl 1 st onto cable needle and hold at front of work; p1; k1 from cable needle.

CKR (CROSS KNIT RIGHT): Sl 1 st onto cable needle and hold at back of work; k1; k1 from cable needle.

CKL (CROSS KNIT LEFT): Sl 1 st onto cable needle and hold at front of work; k1; k1 from cable needle.

C2 (CROSS 2): K 2nd st from the back; then k 1st st from the back.

```
| ✕ | ✕ | • | • | • | • | • | • | ✕ | ✕ | • | • | • | • | • | • | ✕ | ✕ |
| • | C1L |   | • | • | • | • | C1R | C1L |   | • | • | • | • | • | C1R |   | • |
| • | • | ✕ | • | • | • | • | ✕ | • | • | • | • | • | ✕ | • | • |   |   |
| • | • | C1L |   | • | • | C1R |   | • | • | C1L |   | • | • | C1R |   | • | • |
| • | • | • | ✕ | • | • | ✕ | • | • | • | • | ✕ | • | • | ✕ | • | • | • |
| • | • | C1L |   | C1R |   | • | • | • | • | C1L |   | C1R |   | • | • | • | • |
| • | • | • | ✕ | ✕ | • | • | • | • | • | • | ✕ | ✕ | • | • | • | • | • |
| • | • | • | • | C2 |   | • | • | • | • | • | • | C2 |   | • | • | • | • |
| • | • | • | ✕ | ✕ | • | • | • | • | • | • | ✕ | ✕ | • | • | • | • | • |
| • | • | C1R |   | C1L |   | • | • | • | • | C1R |   | C1L |   | • | • | • | • |
| • | • | • | ✕ | • | • | ✕ | • | • | • | • | ✕ | • | • | ✕ | • | • | • |
| • | • | C1R |   | • | • | C1L |   | • | • | C1R |   | • | • | C1L |   | • | • |
| • | • | ✕ | • | • | • | • | ✕ | • | • | ✕ | • | • | • | • | ✕ | • | • |
| C1L |   | C1R |   | • | • | • | • | C1L |   | C1R |   | • | • | • | • | C1L | C1R |
| ✕ | ✕ | • | • | • | • | • | • | ✕ | ✕ | • | • | • | • | • | • | ✕ | ✕ |
| C2 |   | • | • | • | • | • | • | C2 |   | • | • | • | • | • | • | C2 |   |
```

✕ Knit
• Purl

Worked on a multiple of 16 sts plus 2 sts for selvedge (see page 57).

ROW 1: P3, *C2, p6; repeat from * across row, ending p3.

ROW 2: K3, *p2, k6; repeat from * across row, ending k3.

ROW 3: P2, *C1R, C1L, p4; repeat from * across row, ending p2.

ROW 4: K2, *p1, k2, p1, k4; repeat from * across row, ending k2.

ROW 5: P1, *C1R, p2, C1L, p2; repeat from * across row, ending p1.

ROW 6: K1, *p1, k4, p1, k2; repeat from * across row, ending k1.

ROW 7: *C1R, p4, C1L; repeat from * across row.

ROW 8: P1, *k6, p2; repeat from * across row, ending p1.

ROW 9: K1, *p6, C2; repeat from * across row, ending p6, k1.

ROW 10: P1, *k6, p2; repeat from * across row, ending k6, p1.

ROW 11: C1L, *p4, C1R, C1L; repeat from * across row, ending p4, C1R.

ROW 12: K1, *p1, k4, p1, k2; repeat from * across row, ending k1.

ROW 13: P1, *C1L, p2, C1R, p2; repeat from * across row, ending p1.

ROW 14: K2, *p1, k2, p1, k4; repeat from * across row, ending k2.

ROW 15: P2, *C1L, C1R, p4; repeat from * across row, ending p2.

ROW 16: K3, *p2, k6; repeat from * across row, ending k3.

Repeat Rows 1–16 for pattern.

SEA MIST SWEATER

This sweater, with its deep vee and sleeve bands, has the effect of a lattice vest over a ribbed sweater. It may be knitted with two yarns together to give the misty effect, combining two close shades, such as lavender and rose.

SIZES: Small [Medium, Large]

MATERIALS:

Yarn: Lion Brand Bianca
Seven [eight, nine] 40-gram balls *each* of Raspberry and Sea Mist
or
Combination of any 2 fine yarns, such as an acrylic mixture, or sport-weight yarn and mohair, in 2 complementary colors.
NOTE: You will be using 2 balls of yarn at the same time, 1 of each color. The 2 colors may be wound together into ready-to-knit balls, or you may knit the 2 strands simultaneously. Choose the method you prefer.

Needles: Straight knitting needles, U.S. sizes 8 and 10 (Continental sizes 5½ and 6½)
Circular needles, U.S. size 10

70

(Continental size 6½)
Or sizes needed to obtain gauge

Notions: Cable needles, stitch holders, row markers, tapestry needle

GAUGE: With larger needles, in pattern stitch, 15 stitches and 16 rows = 4 inches (10 centimeters)

FINISHED MEASUREMENTS:

Bust: 34 inches (86 centimeters) [38 inches (96.5 centimeters), 42 inches (106.5 centimeters)]

Sleeve (measured at underarm seam): 19 inches (48 centimeters) [20 inches (50.75 centimeters), 21 inches (53.5 centimeters)]

Length: 21 inches (53.5 centimeters) [22 inches (56 centimeters), 23 inches (58.5 centimeters)]

NOTE: For size Small, begin lattice pattern at Row 1. For size Medium, begin lattice pattern at Row 9. For size Large, begin lattice pattern at Row 1.
Refer to page 69 for graph and pattern instructions.
Refer to page 69 for pattern stitch.

BACK

With smaller needles, cast on 64 [72, 80] sts and work in k1, p1 ribbing for 6 rows. Change to larger needles. Work lattice pattern until piece measures 21 inches (53.5 centimeters) [22 inches (56 centimeters), 23 inches (58.5 centimeters)] overall. Bind off 16 [19, 22] sts at beginning of next 2 rows (32 [34, 36] sts). Place remaining sts on holder for neck.

FRONT

Work same as for back until 1½ [2, 2½] diamonds have been completed, ending with pattern Row 10 [Row 2, Row 10] *Begin making vee:*

ROW 11: Work 30 [34, 38] sts in lattice pattern; C1R, C1L; work remaining 30 [34, 38] sts in lattice pattern.

ROW 12: Work 30 [34, 38] sts in lattice pattern; p1, k1, p2; work remaining 30 [34, 38] sts in lattice pattern.

ROW 13: Work 29 [33, 37] sts in lattice pattern; C1R, k1, p1, C1L; work remaining 29 [33, 37] sts in lattice pattern.

ROW 14: Work 29 [33, 37] sts in lattice pattern; p2, k1, p1, k1, p1; work remaining 29 [33, 37] sts in lattice pattern.

Continue increasing the vee in this manner. Work sts inside of vee in k1, p1 ribbing. Work in pattern as established until piece measures 21 inches (53.5 centimeters) [22 inches (56 centimeters), 23 inches (58.5 centimeters)] overall. Bind off 16 [19, 22] sts at beginning of next 2 rows (32 [34, 36] sts). Place remaining sts on holder for neck.

SLEEVE

Work entire sleeve in k1, p1 ribbing. With larger needles, cast on 36 sts and work ribbing for 3 inches (7.5 centimeters).

Shape sleeve: Continue working evenly in ribbing. *At the same time,* inc 1 st, each side, every other row,

until there are 92 [96, 100] sts. Then continue working evenly in ribbing until sleeve measures 19 inches (48 centimeters) [20 inches (50.75 centimeters), 21 inches (53.5 centimeters)] overall.
Bind off loosely.
Work another sleeve in the same manner.

FINISHING

Sew shoulder seams.
Starting at left shoulder, sl front and back sts from holders onto circular needles. Place marker on needle at left shoulder to mark beginning of rounds. Carry marker as you work.

Collar: Work k1, p1 ribbing for 22 rounds, matching k and p to front vee pattern. Bind off collar.

Armhole trim: Place markers on front and back 10 [11, 12] inches down from shoulder seams. With smaller straight needles, pick up 88 [96, 104] sts, evenly spaced, between front and back markers. Work k1, p1 ribbing for 4 rows. *At the same time,* dec 1 st, each side, every row. Bind off.

Sew sleeves to sweater underneath armhole trim so that trim covers seam. Sew sleeve and side seams.

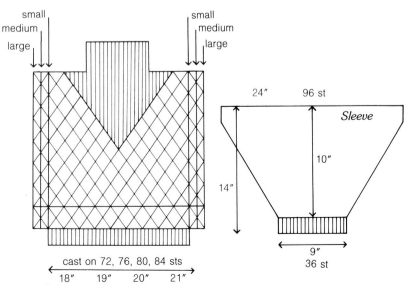

small
medium
large

small
medium
large

24"   96 st

Sleeve

10"

14"

9"
36 st

cast on 72, 76, 80, 84 sts
18"   19"   20"   21"

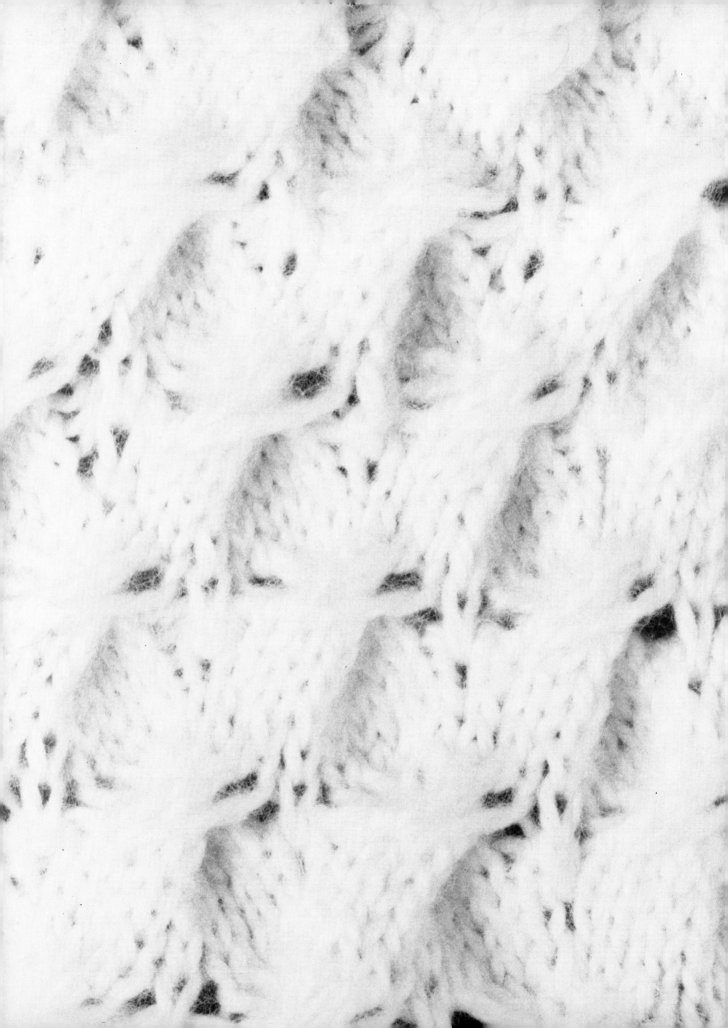

HOW TO MAKE THE LACY CABLE PATTERN

This attractive stitch gives a spider's-web effect when worked with large needles and fine yarn and a sculptured look when worked with medium-sized needles and knitting worsted. Either way, the lacy cable is unique and very satisfying to work once you have mastered it.

The pattern is made on every fifth and sixth row, with four rows of stockinette stitch between. On the fifth row, long loops in groups of seven are formed by wrapping the yarn twice around the needle as each stitch is made. These loops are released on the sixth row to form elongated stitches that are knitted out of order, first in front and then in back, rather like a cable. Between each group of elongated stitches is a single knit stitch. This stitch, the key to the whole pattern, is knitted four stitches *below,* taking the needle from front to back right through the knitting! The stitch on the needle is then dropped, to fall four rows below, where it is stopped by the stitch just taken. This simple technique puts a tuck in the knitting, which makes the raised loops lie evenly and gives the sculptured waffle effect.

Success and ease in working this stitch depend on the size needle you use. In order to make loops long enough to manipulate, you may prefer to use a larger needle just for the fifth row, where the stitches are wrapped. Experiment with different-sized needles and yarns before trying the Lacy Cable Pullover.

Note that as they are being worked, the elongated stitches always look bunched and untidy. Only after the four rows of stockinette stitch between have been knitted does an even twist appear, as if by magic.

This pattern is worked on a multiple of 8 sts, plus 2 selvedge sts. U.S. size 8 (Continental size 5½) needles are recommended for the swatch.

Cast on 30 sts.

ROWS 1 AND 3: Knit.

ROWS 2 AND 4: Purl.

ROW 5: P3; *p1; p7, wrapping the yarn lightly *twice* around the needle as you take each purl st (these sts will be referred to below as *elongated sts*); repeat from * across row, ending p3.

ROW 6: K3; insert point of right needle at base of each of the 7 elongated sts and sl each one over, letting the loops go as you slide them over to the right needle. Next, slide left needle through all 7 of these loops and begin lace-knitting with the right needle. Pass the needle in front of the work and pick up the 7th elongated st (the farthest from the tip of the needle), knitwise. Lift it to bring it close to the tip, k it, but do not slide it off the needle. Repeat for 6th, 5th, and 4th sts. (It is helpful to separate the sts with your thumb as you work.) Still holding sts on needle, swing needle to back of work and k 3rd, then 2nd, and then 1st st. (To do this, hold the needle almost vertically and slide it between sts, again separating them with your thumb.) Now drop all 7 sts off the left needle. The next st on the left needle is a k st. Instead of knitting it, plunge the needle straight through the knitting, 4 sts directly below, and pull through a loop as if to k. Now drop k st off the needle—it will not drop past st you have just made. This completes 1 pattern motif. Repeat across row, ending k3.

ROWS 6 AND 8: Purl.

ROWS 7 AND 9: Knit.

ROW 10: P2; *work 4 elongated sts, p1, work 3 elongated sts; repeat from * across row, ending 4 elongated sts, p2.

ROW 11: P2; *cross elongated sts, k the k sts, inserting needle in corresponding sts 4 rows below; repeat from * across row, ending k2. At beginning and end of row, cross sts in pairs (this makes the lacy cable motifs alternate, brick-fashion, over the whole area, instead of lining up each directly above previous raised cable).

ROWS 12 AND 14: Purl.

ROWS 13 AND 15: Knit.

Repeat from Row 4 for pattern.

Pulling out the extra "wrap" to give 7 elongated stitches on the right needle

Transferring 7 elongated stitches to the left needle

Passing the needle in front of work, knitting the 7th stitch, then the 6th, then the 5th, then the 4th, without dropping them off the needle

74

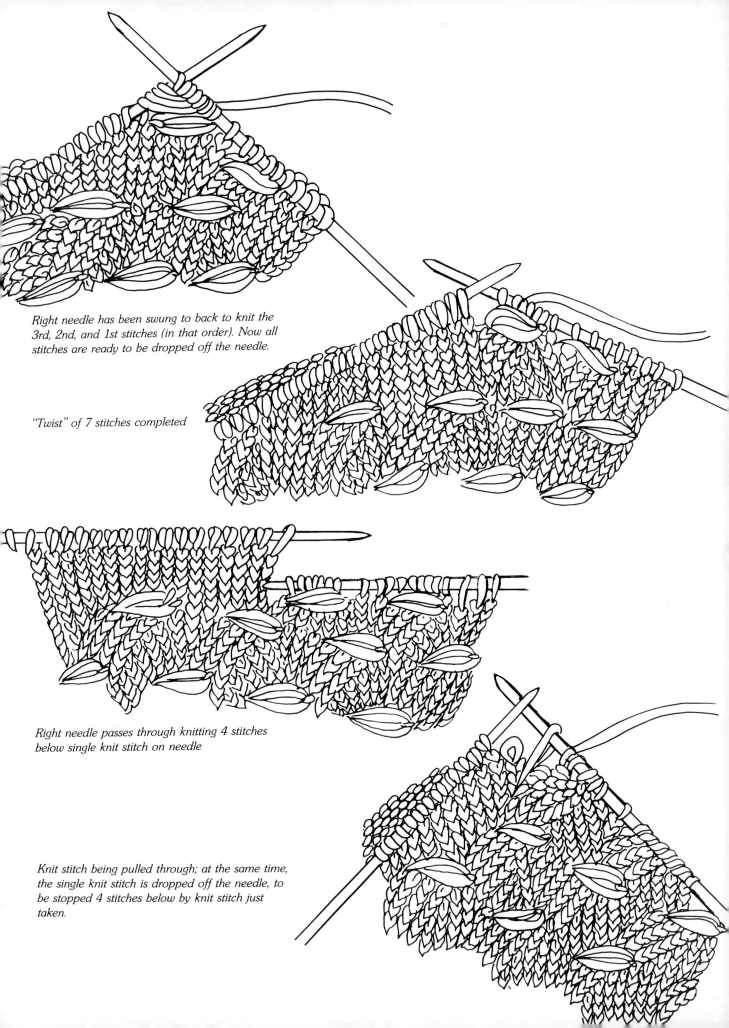

Right needle has been swung to back to knit the 3rd, 2nd, and 1st stitches (in that order). Now all stitches are ready to be dropped off the needle.

"Twist" of 7 stitches completed

Right needle passes through knitting 4 stitches below single knit stitch on needle

Knit stitch being pulled through; at the same time, the single knit stitch is dropped off the needle, to be stopped 4 stitches below by knit stitch just taken.

LACY CABLE PULLOVER
(Color photo page 47)

This airy, lightweight sweater is also very warm, because of the stitch construction. A variegated yarn is particularly attractive with this pattern, which highlights glints of color.

SIZES: Small [Medium]

MATERIALS:

Yarn: 8 [10] balls of Anny Blatt's Starblitz Uranus (charcoal gray) (60% mohair, 20% polyamide, 20% Courtelle)

or

Silk and wool tweed

or

Lopi-light worsted weight

Needles: Straight knitting needles, U.S. sizes 7, 8, 9, and 10½ (Continental sizes 5, 5½, 6, and 7) *Or sizes needed to obtain gauge*

GAUGE: With largest needles, in pattern, 16 stitches and 14 rows = 4 inches (10 centimeters)

FINISHED MEASUREMENTS:

Bust: 42½ inches (108 centimeters) [46½ inches (118 centimeters)]

Sleeve (measured at underarm seam): 18½ inches (47 centimeters) [19 inches (48 centimeters)]

Length: 25 inches (63.5 centimeters) [25¾ inches (65.5 centimeters)]

Refer to page 73 for pattern stitch.

BACK

With smallest needles, cast on 80 [84] sts and work in k2, p2 ribbing for 5½ inches (14 centimeters).

Change to largest needles. Working in pattern, inc 5 [9] sts across first row, evenly spaced (85 [93] sts). Work evenly until back measures 15 inches (38 centimeters) [15½ inches (39.5 centimeters)].

Shape armholes: Bind off, at each side, 4 [5] sts once (77 [83] sts). Keeping in pattern, continue to work evenly until back measures 24¾ inches (63.75 centimeters) [25½ inches (65 centimeters)] overall.

Shape shoulders: Bind off, at each side, every other row, 11 [12] sts twice (33 [35] sts). Then bind off remaining sts for neck.

FRONT

Work same as for back until front measures 22½ inches (57 centimeters) [23¼ inches (59 centimeters)] overall.

Shape neck: Bind off center 17 [19] sts and continue each side separately. Bind off at neck edge, every other row, 4 sts once, 3 sts once, and 1 st once (22 [24] sts). Be sure to keep pattern correct while shaping. When front measures 24¾ inches (63.75 centimeters) [25½ inches (65 centimeters)] overall,

Shape shoulders: as for back.

SLEEVE

With smallest needles, cast on 40 [44] sts and work in k2, p2 ribbing for 4½ inches (11.5 centimeters). Change to largest needles. Working in pattern, inc 13 sts, evenly spaced, across first row (53 [57] sts). For size Small, begin with Row 4 of pattern as established. For size Medium, begin 4th row of pattern as follows: P2; 2 elongated sts; *p1, 7 elongated sts; continue from * as established.

Shape sleeve: Inc 1 st, each side, every other row, 6 times, then every 6th row, 6 times (77 [81] sts). Work until sleeve measures 18½ inches (47 centimeters) [19 inches (48 centimeters)] overall.

Shape cap: Bind off, at each side, every other row, 5 sts 3 times (47 [51] sts).

Bind off remaining sts.

Work another sleeve in the same manner.

FINISHING

Join right shoulder seam.

Collar: RS facing, with smallest needles, pick up 108 [114] sts, evenly spaced, along neck edge. Change to next needle size (U.S. 8; Continental 5½) and work in k3, p3 ribbing for 2¾ inches (7 centimeters). Change to next needle size (U.S. 9; Continental 6) and work in k3, p3 ribbing for 5½ inches (14 centimeters) more.

Bind off in ribbing.

Join left shoulder seam.

Close collar.

Set sleeves in.

Join side and sleeve seams.

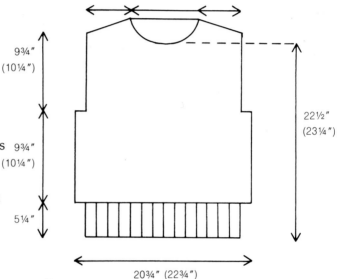

5½" (5¾") 7¾" (8¼") 5½" (5¾")

9¾"
(10¼")

9¾"
(10¼")

5¼"

22½"
(23¼")

20¾" (22¾")

Back and Front

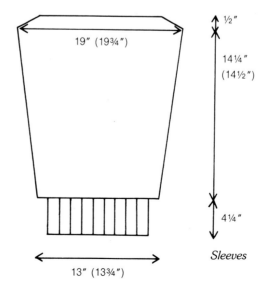

19" (19¾")

½"

14¼"
(14½")

4¼"

13" (13¾")

Sleeves

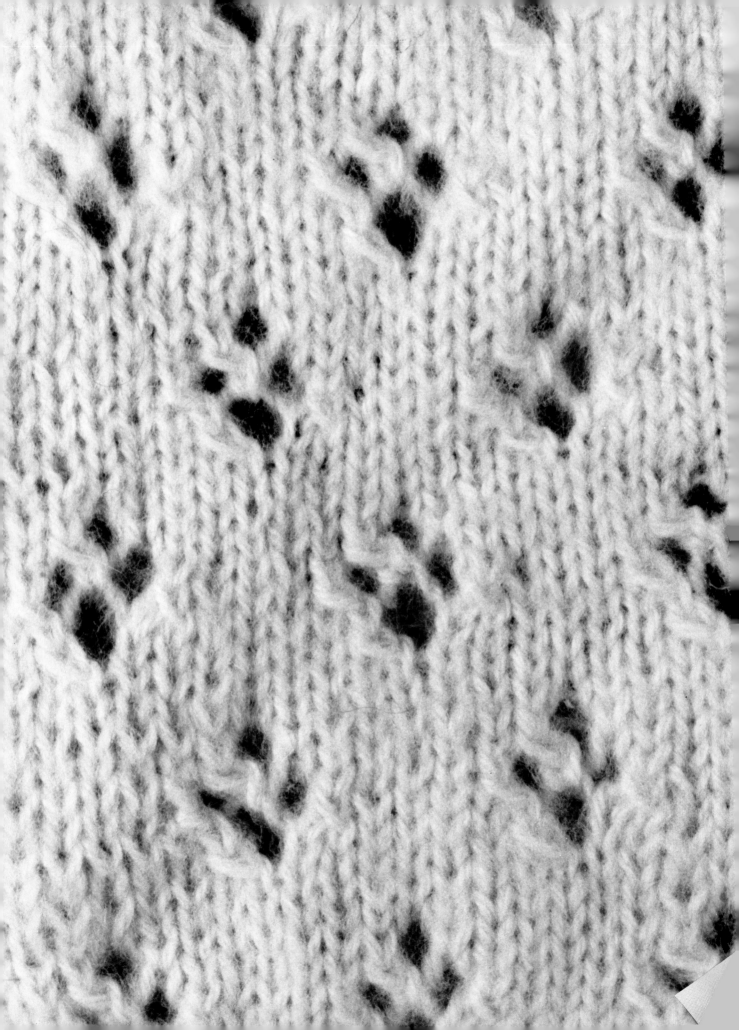

HOW TO MAKE EYELET LACE

Like the more intricate lace leaves design (see page 88), these eyelets are made on the simple principle of winding yarn around the needle to make an extra stitch and then making up for the extra stitch by knitting two stitches together.

When the stitch before the increase is a knit stitch and the stitch that follows is a knit stitch, use *yf.* For yf, the yarn is brought forward under the needle and then brought over the needle to the back again.

When the stitch before the increase is a purl stitch and the stitch that follows is to be purled, use *yrn.* For yrn, bring the yarn over the right needle and then under again from back to front.

When the stitch before the increase is a purl stitch but the stitch that follows is to be knitted, and vice versa, use *yon.* For yon, the yarn must be brought back under the needle, then wrapped around over the needle to the front and under to the back again.

FOUR-LEAF CLOVER EYELET LACE
The eyelets are grouped together in blocks of 4. This pattern is worked in multiples of 8 sts over 16 rows.

ROW 1 AND ALL ALTERNATE ROWS: Purl.
ROW 2: Knit.
ROW 4: K3; *yf, sl1, k1, psso, k6; repeat from * across row, ending k3.
ROW 6: K1; *k 2 tog, yf, k1, yf, sl1, k1, psso, k3; repeat from * across row, ending k2.
ROW 8: Repeat Row 4.

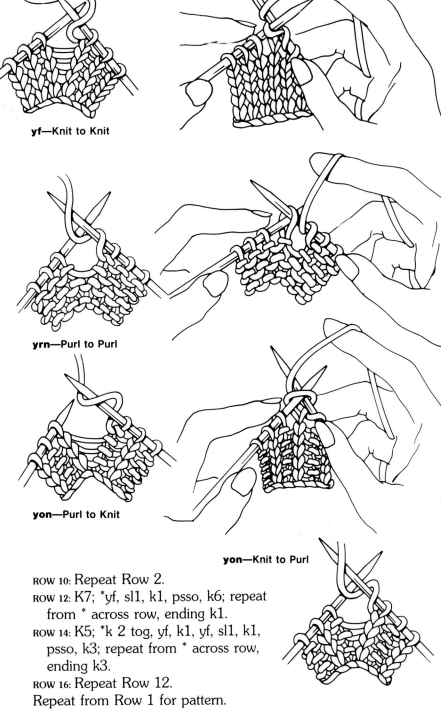

yf—Knit to Knit

yrn—Purl to Purl

yon—Purl to Knit

yon—Knit to Purl

ROW 10: Repeat Row 2.
ROW 12: K7; *yf, sl1, k1, psso, k6; repeat from * across row, ending k1.
ROW 14: K5; *k 2 tog, yf, k1, yf, sl1, k1, psso, k3; repeat from * across row, ending k3.
ROW 16: Repeat Row 12.
Repeat from Row 1 for pattern.

PINAFORE
(Color photo page 78)

This charming eyelet-lace pinafore could be worn over a fabric dress, but the knitted Classic Dress is the perfect foil for it.

SIZES: Child's 1 [3, 6, 8]

MATERIALS:

Yarn: Two [three, three, three] 1¾-ounce (50-gram) balls of white Emu Superwash or Bambino Raindrop

Needles: Straight knitting needles, U.S. sizes 4 and 5 (Continental sizes 3¾ and 4)

Or sizes needed to obtain gauge

Notions: Stitch holder, tapestry needle, prefinished eyelet-lace edging

GAUGE: With larger needles, in stockinette stitch, 11 stitches = 2 inches (5 centimeters), 31 rows = 4 inches (10 centimeters)

SKIRT

With smaller needles, cast on 80 sts and work 4 rows St st. Change to larger needles.

PICOT ROW: K1; *k 2 tog, yf; repeat from * to last st; k1. Beginning with p row, work 5 rows St st. Proceed in pattern as follows:

ROW 1 (RS): K3; *yon, sl1, k1, psso, k6; repeat from * across row, ending k3.

ROW 2 (AND ALL FOLLOWING ALTERNATE ROWS): Purl.

ROW 3: K1; *k 2 tog, yf, k1, yon, sl1, k1, psso, k3; repeat from * across row, ending k2.

ROW 5: Repeat Row 1.

ROW 7: Knit.

ROW 9: K7; *yon, sl1, k1, psso, k6; repeat from * across until 1 st remains, k1.

ROW 11: K5; *k 2 tog, yf, k1, yon, sl1, k1, psso, k3; repeat from * across row until 3 sts remain, k3.

ROW 13: Repeat Row 9.

ROW 15: Knit.

ROW 16: Purl.

Repeat these 16 rows until skirt measures 10½ inches (26.5 centimeters) [13 inches (33 centimeters), 15½ inches (39.5 centimeters), 15½ inches (39.5 centimeters)] overall, ending on Row 8 or Row 16.

DEC ROW: K10; (k 2 tog) 30 times; k10 (50 sts). P 1 row. Then cast on 80 sts at beginning of next 2 rows for waist ties (210 sts). Work 1 inch (2.5 centimeters) garter st. Bind off 82 sts at beginning of next 2 rows (46 sts). Do not cut yarn: Continue with bodice.

BODICE

NEXT ROW: K7; turn work; leave remaining sts on holder. Work 23 inches (58.5 centimeters) garter st for strap. Bind off. Put sts from holder onto needle. Join yarn to inner end of holder sts, k32; turn work; put remaining 7 sts back on holder. Beginning with p row, work 3 rows St st. Work in pattern as for skirt for 5 inches (12.5 centimeters), ending with p row. Bind off. Place remaining 7 sts from holder onto needle. Rejoin yarn and work 23 inches (58.5 centimeters) garter st for strap.
Bind off.

FINISHING

Sew straps to side of bodice. Sew hem in place. Fold ends of straps to form loops and sew in position; then thread waist ties through loops. Sew prefinished eyelet-lace edging down side edges of skirt and across top of bodice.

CHILD'S VICTORIAN YOKE DRESS

(Photo page 79)

Like the Child's Classic Dress on page 78, this charming, easy-fitting dress can be knitted as a complete costume, or the yoke and banding at shoulders and hem can be added to a fabric dress.

SIZES: Child's 1 [3, 6, 8]

MATERIALS:

Yarn: 1¾-ounce (50-gram) balls of Emu Superwash wool or Bambino Raindrop acrylic

    5 [6, 6, 7] balls of maroon (*A*)

    2 [2, 2, 2] balls of white (*B*)

Needles: Straight knitting needles, U.S. sizes 3 and 5 (Continental sizes 3¼ and 4)

    Or sizes needed to obtain gauge

Notions: 1 yard (1 meter) maroon velvet ribbon, stitch holders, row counters, tapestry needle

GAUGE: With larger needles, in stockinette stitch, 11 stitches = 2 inches (5 centimeters), 31 rows = 4 inches (10 centimeters)

FINISHED MEASUREMENTS:

Chest: 20 inches (50.75 centimeters) [22 inches (56 centimeters), 24 inches (61 centimeters), 26 inches (66 centimeters)]

Length: 22 inches (56 centimeters) [24½ inches (62.25 centimeters), 27 inches (68.5 centimeters), 29 inches (73.5 centimeters)]

Sleeve (measured at underarm seam): 8 inches (20 centimeters) [9½ inches (24 centimeters), 10½ inches (26.5

centimeters), 11½ inches (29.25
centimeters)]

BACK
Right back: With smaller needles and
color A, cast on 45 [47, 51, 53] sts
and work k1, p1 ribbing for 4 rows.
For sizes 3 and 8 only, inc 1 st at
center of last row (45 [48, 51, 54]
sts). Change to larger needles and
work evenly in St st until back
measures 16 inches (40.5 centimeters)
[18½ inches (47 centimeters), 21
inches (53.5 centimeters), 23 inches
(58.5 centimeters)] overall, ending on
p row. Mark end of last row with
colored thread.
Shape raglan: Dec 1 st at beginning of
next row and at this same edge every
row until 41 [44, 47, 50] sts remain,
ending on p row. Cut off yarn. Put
remaining stitches on holder.
Left back: Work same as for right back,
except end on k row and mark row
before shaping raglan.

FRONT
Using smaller needles and color A, cast
on 89 [95, 101, 107] sts and work k1,
p1 ribbing for 4 rows, increasing 1 st at
center of last row for all sizes (90 [96,
102, 108] sts). Change to larger needles.
Work evenly in St st until front
measures 16 inches (40.5 centimeters)
[18½ inches (47 centimeters), 21 inches
(53.5 centimeters), 23 inches (58.5
centimeters)] overall, ending on p row.
(Length can be adjusted here.) Mark
ends of last row with colored thread.
Shape raglan: Dec 1 st, each side, next
4 rows (82 [88, 94, 100] sts). Cut off
yarn and put remaining sts on holder.

SLEEVE
With smaller needles and color A, cast

84

on 36 [36, 38, 38] sts and work k1, p1
ribbing for 1½ inches (3.75 centimeters).
INC ROW: Rib 4 [1, 4, 6]; *work twice into
next st, rib 2 [2, 2, 1]; repeat from *
to last 5 [2, 4, 6] sts; work twice into
next st, rib to end (46 [48, 49, 52]
sts). Change to larger needles. Work
evenly in St st until sleeve measures 8
inches (20 centimeters) [9½ inches
(24 centimeters), 10½ inches (26.5
centimeters), 11½ inches (29.25
centimeters)] overall, ending on p row.
(Length can be adjusted here.) Mark
each end of last row with colored
thread.
Shape top: Dec 1 st, each side, next 4
rows (38 [40, 41, 44] sts). P 1 row.
Cut off yarn and put remaining sts on
holder.
Work another sleeve in the same
manner.

YOKE
With RS facing, join color A to left back
sts on holder, and, with larger needles, k
sts as follows: (K1, k 2 tog) 9 [10, 11, 9]
times; (k1, k3 tog) 3 [3, 3, 5] times; k2
[2, 2, 3]; k 1st sleeve sts: (k1, k 2 tog)
12 [13, 13, 14] times; k2 [1, 2, 2]; k sts
from front holder as follows: (k1, k 2
tog) 12 [11, 12, 13] times, k1 [2, 2, 1],
(k 3 tog) 3 [5, 5, 7] times, (k1, k 2 tog)
11 [12, 13, 12] times, k3 [2, 2, 3]; work
sts of 2nd sleeve as for 1st sleeve; work
right back sts from holder as follows: k2
[2, 2, 3], (k 3 tog, k1) 3 [3, 3, 5] times,
(k 2 tog, k1) 9 [10, 11, 9] times (157
[165, 175, 183] sts). K 3 rows. Cut off
color A; join color B. Work 2 [2, 4, 4]
rows in St st.
ROW 1: K5 [6, 8, 8]; *yon, sl1, k1, psso, k8
[8, 9, 9]; repeat from * to last 12 [9,
13, 10] sts; yon, sl1, k1, psso, k to
end.
ROW 2 AND ALL ALTERNATE ROWS: Purl.
ROW 3: K3 [4, 6, 6]; *k 2 tog, yf, k1, yon,

sl1, k1, psso, k5 [5, 6, 6]; repeat from * to last 4 [1, 4, 1] sts, k to end.

ROW 5: Repeat Row 1.

ROW 7 (DEC ROW): K8 [9, 11, 11]; *k 2 tog, k8 [8, 9, 9]; repeat from * to last 9 [16, 10, 18] sts; k 2 tog, k to end (142 [150, 160, 168] sts).

ROW 9: K5 [6, 8, 8]; *yon, sl1, k1, psso, k7 [7, 8, 8]; repeat from * to last 11 [9, 12, 10] sts; yon, sl1, k1, psso, k to end.

ROW 11: K3 [4, 6, 6]; *k2 tog, yf, k1, yon, sl1, k1, psso, k4 [4, 5, 5]; repeat from * to last 13 [11, 14, 12] sts; k 2 tog, yf, k1, yon, sl1, k1, psso, k to end.

ROW 13: Repeat Row 9.

ROW 15 (DEC ROW): K8 [9, 11, 11]; *k 2 tog, k7 [7, 8, 8]; repeat from * to last 7 [15, 9, 17] sts; k 2 tog, k to end (127 [135, 145, 153] sts).

ROW 17: K5 [6, 8, 8]; *yon, sl1, k1, psso, k6 [6, 7, 7]; repeat from * to last 10 [9, 11, 10] sts; yon, sl1, k1, psso, k to end.

ROW 19: K3 [4, 6, 6]; *k 2 tog, yf, k1, yon, sl1, k1, psso, k3 [3, 4, 4]; repeat from * to last 12 [11, 13, 12] sts; k 2 tog, yf, k1, yon, sl1, k1, psso, k to end.

ROW 21: Repeat Row 17.

ROW 23 (DEC ROW): K8 [9, 11, 11]; *k 2 tog, k6 [6, 7, 7]; repeat from * to last 7 [14, 8, 16] sts; k 2 tog, k to end (112 [120, 130, 138] sts).

ROW 25: K5 [6, 8, 8]; *yon, sl1, k1, psso, k5 [5, 6, 6]; repeat from * to last 9 [9, 10, 10] sts; yon, sl1, k1, psso, k to end.

ROW 27: K3 [4, 6, 6]; *k 2 tog, yo, k1, yon, sl1, k1, psso, k2 [2, 3, 3]; repeat from * to last 11 [11, 12, 12] sts; k 2 tog, yo, k1, yon, sl1, k1, psso, k to end.

ROW 29: Repeat Row 25.

ROW 31 (DEC ROW): K8 [9, 11, 11]; *k 2 tog, k5 [5, 6, 6]; repeat from * to last 6 [13, 7, 15] sts; k 2 tog, k to end (97 [105, 115, 123] sts).

Beginning with p row, work 3 rows St

st. Change to smaller needles and work 2 rows ribbing.

Eyelet-hole row: Rib 2; (k 2 tog, yf, rib 2) 23 [25, 27, 30] times; k 2 tog, yf, rib to end. Work 3 more rows ribbing.

Picot edging: Bind off 2; *sl st used in binding off back onto left needle, cast on 2, then bind off 4; repeat from * to last st; bind off last st.

YOKE BORDER

Using smaller needles and color B, cast on 4 sts. FOUNDATION ROW: K.

ROW 1 (RS): K1, yon, sl1, k1, psso, yo, k1 (5 sts).

ROW 2: P1, yf, p1, p 2 tog, yon, k1 (6 sts).

ROW 3: K1, yon, sl1, k1, psso, yo, k 2 tog, yo, k1 (7 sts).

ROW 4: P1, yrn, p 2 tog, yrn, p 2 tog, yon, k1 (8 sts).

ROW 5: K1, yon, sl1, k1, psso, k1, yf, k 2 tog, k2 (8 sts).

ROW 6: Bind off 4, p 2 tog, yon, k1 (4 sts).

Repeat from Row 1 to Row 6 until border, slightly stretched, fits all around garter st ridge of yoke, ending on 6th row.

Bind off.

HEM BORDER

With larger needles and color B, cast on 4 sts. Work as for yoke border until border, slightly stretched, fits all around lower edge.

FINISHING

Join raglan sleeves, matching colored-thread markers, then join side and sleeve seams. Join center back and yoke seam. Join yoke edging seam and sew to 1st row of ridge on yoke. Join hem edging and sew to underside of ribbing at hemline. Cut ribbon in half; attach to each side of back neck; then thread through eyelet holes at neck.

CHILD'S CLASSIC DRESS
(Photo page 78)

SIZES: Child's 1 [3, 6, 8]

MATERIALS:
Yarn: 1¾-ounce (50-gram) balls of Emu Superwash
    5 [6, 6, 7] balls of navy *or* peony red
    1 ball of white (for collar)
Needles: Straight knitting needles, U.S. sizes 3, 4, and 5 (Continental sizes 3¼, 3¾, and 4)
Or sizes needed to obtain gauge
Notions: 4 buttons, prefinished eyelet-lace edging, st holder, safety pin

GAUGE: With largest needles, in stockinette stitch, 11 stitches = 2 inches (5 centimeters), 31 rows = 4 inches (10 centimeters)

FINISHED MEASUREMENTS:
Chest: 20 inches (50.75 cm) [22 inches (56 cm), 24 inches (61 cm), 26 inches (66 cm)]
Length: 24½ inches (62.25 cm) [27 inches (68.5 cm), 30½ inches (77.5 cm), 31½ inches (80 cm)]
Sleeve (measured at underarm seam): 8 inches (20 cm) [9½ inches (24 cm), 10½ inches (26.5 cm), 11½ inches (29.25 cm)]

BACK
With medium-sized needles, cast on 92 [96, 102, 108] sts and work 4 rows St st. Change to largest needles.

Picot row: K1, *yf, k 2 tog. Repeat from * to end of row. P next row. Work evenly in St st until back measures 15 inches (38 cm) [16½ inches (42 cm), 19 inches (48 cm), 19 inches (48 cm)] overall, ending with a p row. (Length can be adjusted here.)

Dec row: K1 [3, 6, 9] sts, (k 2 tog, k1) 30 times, k1 [3, 6, 9] (62 [66, 72, 78] sts).
Beginning with p row, work evenly in St st for 5 inches (12.5 cm) [5½ inches (14 cm), 6 inches (15.25 cm), 6½ inches (16.5 cm)] more, ending with a p row.

Shape armholes: Cast off 2 [3, 3, 4] sts at beg of next 2 rows, then dec 1 st each end of next and every following alternate row until 50 [52, 56, 58] sts remain.* Work straight until armholes measure 2 inches (5 cm) [2¼ inches (5.5 cm), 2½ inches (6.25 cm), 2¾ inches (7 cm)] from beg of shaping, ending p row.

Divide for back opening: K28 [30, 33, 36]. Put remaining sts on holder. Turn work.
Work evenly in St st until back measures 4½ inches (11.5 cm) [5 inches (12.5 cm), 5½ inches (14 cm), 6 inches (15.25 cm)] from beginning of shaping. End at armhole edge.

Shape shoulder: Bind off 7 [7, 8, 8] sts at beginning of next row, and 7 sts at beginning of following alternate row. Work 1 row. Bind off. Take sts off holder. With RS facing, sl first 6 sts onto a safety pin. Join yarn to next st and k to end of row.
Complete to match other side.

FRONT
Work as for back until 50 [52, 56, 58]

sts remain as armholes are being shaped. Continue evenly in St st until armholes measure 3 inches (7.5 cm) [3½ inches (9 cm), 4 inches (10 cm), 4½ inches (11.5 cm)] from beginning of shaping, ending with p row.

Divide for neck: K19 [20, 21, 22] sts. Put remaining sts on holder. Turn work. Dec 1 st at neck edge, every row, until 14 [14, 15, 15] sts remain. Work evenly in St st until armhole measures 4½ inches (11.5 cm) [5 inches (12.5 cm), 5½ inches (14 cm), 6 inches (15.25 cm)] from beginning of armhole shaping. End at armhole edge.

Shape shoulder: Bind off 7 [7, 8, 8] sts at beginning of next row. Work 1 row. Bind off. Take sts off holder. With RS facing, join on yarn and bind off first 12 [12, 14, 14] sts, k to end of row. Complete to match other side of neck.

SLEEVE

With medium-sized needles, cast on 36 [36, 38, 38] sts and work k1, p1 ribbing for 1½ inches (3.75 cm).

INC ROW: Rib 4 [1, 2, 4] sts; *work twice into next st, rib 2 [2, 2, 1] st; repeat from * to last 5 [2, 3, 4] sts; work twice into next st; rib to end (46 [48, 50, 54] sts). Change to largest needles. Work evenly in St st until sleeve measures 8 inches (20 cm) [9½ inches (24 cm), 10½ inches (26.5 cm), 11½ inches (29.25 cm)] overall. End with a p row. (Length can be adjusted here.)

Shape top: Bind off 2 [3, 3, 4] sts at beginning of next 2 rows. Dec 1 st, each side, next and every following 4th row until 30 [28, 30, 30] sts remain. Then dec 1 st, each side, every following alternate row until 26 [22, 18, 18] sts remain. Now dec 1 st, each side, every row, until 12 sts remain.

Bind off. Work another sleeve in the same manner.

NECKBAND

Join shoulder seams. With RS facing, join yarn to left side for back neck, and, using medium-sized needles, pick up and k 8 [9, 10, 11] sts from LS of back neck, 11 sts down left front neck, 12 [12, 14, 14] sts from front neck, 11 sts up right front neck, and 8 [9, 10, 11] sts from right side of back neck (50 [52, 56, 58] sts). Beginning with p row, work 3 rows St st.

PICOT ROW: K1; *yf, k 2 tog; repeat from * to last st; k1. Beginning with p row, work 3 rows St st. Bind off. Fold neckband to WS and sew in place.

BUTTON BORDER

With largest needles, cast on 6 sts and work garter st until border, slightly stretched, fits up back neck opening to top of neck edging. Bind off. Sew border onto dress. Mark 4 button positions on border, the 1st one ½ inch (1.25 centimeters) from cast-on edge, the top one ½ inch (1.25 centimeters) from bound-off edge, and the others spaced evenly between.

BUTTONHOLE BORDER

Take 6 sts off safety pin. With RS facing, join on yarn and k these 6 sts. Work border as for button border, but make buttonholes in line with button markers as follows:

BUTTONHOLE ROW (RS): K2, k 2 tog, yf, k2. Sew border onto dress.

FINISHING

Run a thread around the sleeve top and ease into armhole. Sew in place. Join side and sleeve seams. Turn up hem and sew in place. Sew on buttons.

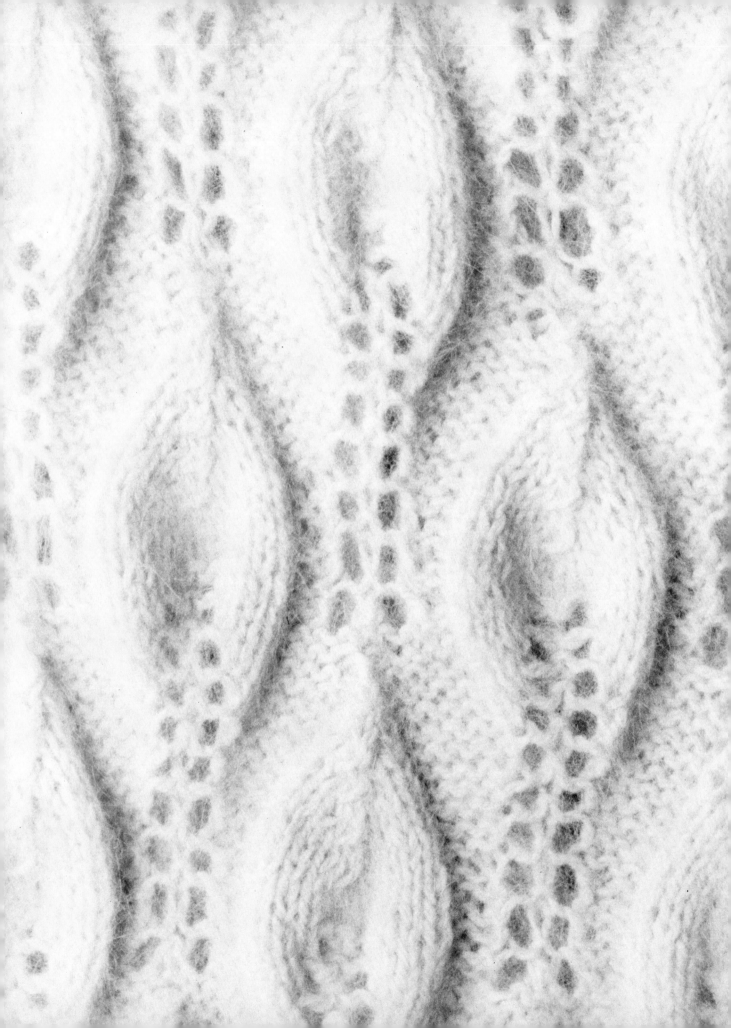

HOW TO MAKE THE LACE LEAVES PATTERN

Lace-knitting techniques appear complex, but once a few basic terms have been mastered, they are amazingly simple. By increasing, decreasing, slipping stitches, and knitting them together, you can form most interesting openwork effects. This version of lace knitting is quite intricate. For a less challenging pattern to begin with, try the Four-Leaf Clover on page 81.

The lace leaves pattern is worked on multiples of 20 stitches. To form a complete leaf at the seam when using straight needles, you must knit half a leaf at each side of the pattern pieces. Because 3 stitches are knitted together at the center of each leaf, and 3 is not divisible by 2, you must add an extra stitch to the total number you cast on. This will allow you to knit 2 together on each side of the pattern piece to make the half-leaf motif. To knit a swatch with the minimum number of repeats, you should therefore cast on 41 stitches. The chart makes this clear (see page 91).

The pattern is knitted with predominantly purl stitches forming the right side. Therefore, the pattern starts on the wrong, or reverse, side. Start reading the chart on the left, and work back and forth, left to right, right to left, left to right, and so on, from the bottom up. For easy reading, place the chart on a metal board and move a magnetized strip along as you work to keep your place.

This pattern is worked on a multiple of 20 sts, plus 1 st (there are no selvedge sts).

ROW 1 (WS): P6; *k2, sl1, k1, psso, yo, k1, yo, k 2 tog, k2, p11; repeat from * across row, ending p6.

ROW 2: K6; *p9, k11; repeat from * across row, ending k6.

ROW 3: P6; *k2, k 2 tog, yo, k1, yo, sl1, k1, psso, k2, p11; repeat from * across row, ending p6.

ROW 4: Repeat Row 2.

ROW 5: P 2 tog; *p4, k4, yo, k1, yo, k4, p4, p 3 tog; repeat from * across row, ending p 2 tog.

ROW 6: K5; *p11, k9; repeat from * across row, ending k5.

ROW 7: P 2 tog; *p3, k5, yo, k1, yo, k5, p3, p 3 tog; repeat from * across row, ending p 2 tog.

ROW 8: K4; *p13, k7; repeat from * across row, ending k4.

ROW 9: P 2 tog; *p2, k6, yo, k1, yo, k6, p2, p 3 tog; repeat from * across row, ending p 2 tog.

ROW 10: K3; *p15, k5; repeat from * across row, ending k3.

ROW 11: P 2 tog; *p1, k6, p1, yo, k1, yo, p1, k6, p1, p 3 tog; repeat from * across row, ending p 2 tog.

ROW 12: K2; *p6, k1, p3, k1, p6, k3; repeat from * across row, ending k2.

ROW 13: P 2 tog; *k6, p2, yo, k1, yo, p2, k6, p 3 tog; repeat from * across row, ending p 2 tog.

ROW 14: K1; *p6, k2, p3, k2, p3, k2, p6, k1; repeat from * across row.

ROW 15: K 2 tog; *k5, p3, yo, k1, yo, p3, k5, sl1, k 2 tog, psso; repeat from * across row, ending sl1, k1, psso.

ROW 16: P6, *k3, p3, k3, p11; repeat from * across row, ending p6.

ROW 17: Sl1, k1, psso, *yo, k 2 tog, k2, p4, yo, k1, yo, p4, k2, sl1, k1, psso, yo,

sl1, k 2 tog, psso; repeat from *
across row, ending k 2 tog.

ROW 18: P5, *k4, p3, k4, p9; repeat from *
across row, ending p5.

ROW 19: K1, *yo, k 2 tog, k2, p11, k2, sl1,
k1, psso, yo, k1; repeat from * across
row.

ROW 20: P5, *k11, p9; repeat from *
across row, ending p5.

ROW 21: K1; *yo, sl1, k1, psso, k2, p11,
k2, k 2 tog, yo, k1; repeat from *
across row, ending k1.

ROW 22: Repeat Row 20.

ROW 23: K1, *yo, k4, p4, p 3 tog, p4, k4,
yo, k1; repeat from * across row.

ROW 24: P6; *k9, p11; repeat from *
across row, ending p6.

ROW 25: K1; *yo, k5, p3, p 3 tog, p3, k5,
yo, k1; repeat from * across row.

ROW 26: P7; *k7, p13; repeat from *
across row, ending p7.

ROW 27: K1; *yo, k6, p2, p 3 tog, p2, k6,
yo, k1; repeat from * across row.

ROW 28: P8; *k5, p15; repeat from *
across row, ending p8.

ROW 29: K1; *yo, p1, k6, p1, p 3 tog, p1,
k6, p1, yo, k1; repeat from * across
row.

ROW 30: P2; *k1, p6, k3, p6, k1, p3; repeat
from * across row, ending p2.

ROW 31: K1; *yo, p2, k6, p 3 tog, p1, k6,
p2, yo, k1; repeat from * across row.

ROW 32: P2; *k2, p6, k1, p6, k2, p3; repeat
from * across row, ending p2.

ROW 33: K1; *yo, p3, k5, sl1, k 2 tog, psso,
k5, p3, yo, k1; repeat from * across
row.

ROW 34: P2; *k3, p11, k3, p3; repeat from
* across row, ending p2.

ROW 35: K1; *yo, p4, k2, sl1, k1, psso, yo,
sl1, k 2 tog, psso, yo, k 2 tog, k2, p4,
yo, k1; repeat from * across row.

ROW 36: P2; *k4, p9, k4, p3; repeat from *
across row, ending p2.

Repeat from Row 1 for pattern.

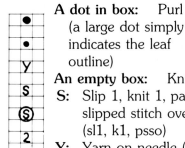

A dot in box: Purl
(a large dot simply
indicates the leaf
outline)

An empty box: Knit

S: Slip 1, knit 1, pass
slipped stitch over
(sl1, k1, psso)

Y: Yarn on needle (yon),
or yarn over (yo)

2: Knit *or* purl 2 together
(k 2 tog *or* p 2 tog)

3: Purl 3 together (p 3 tog)

S in a circle: Slip 1, knit 2
together, pass slip
stitch over (sl1, k 2 tog, psso)

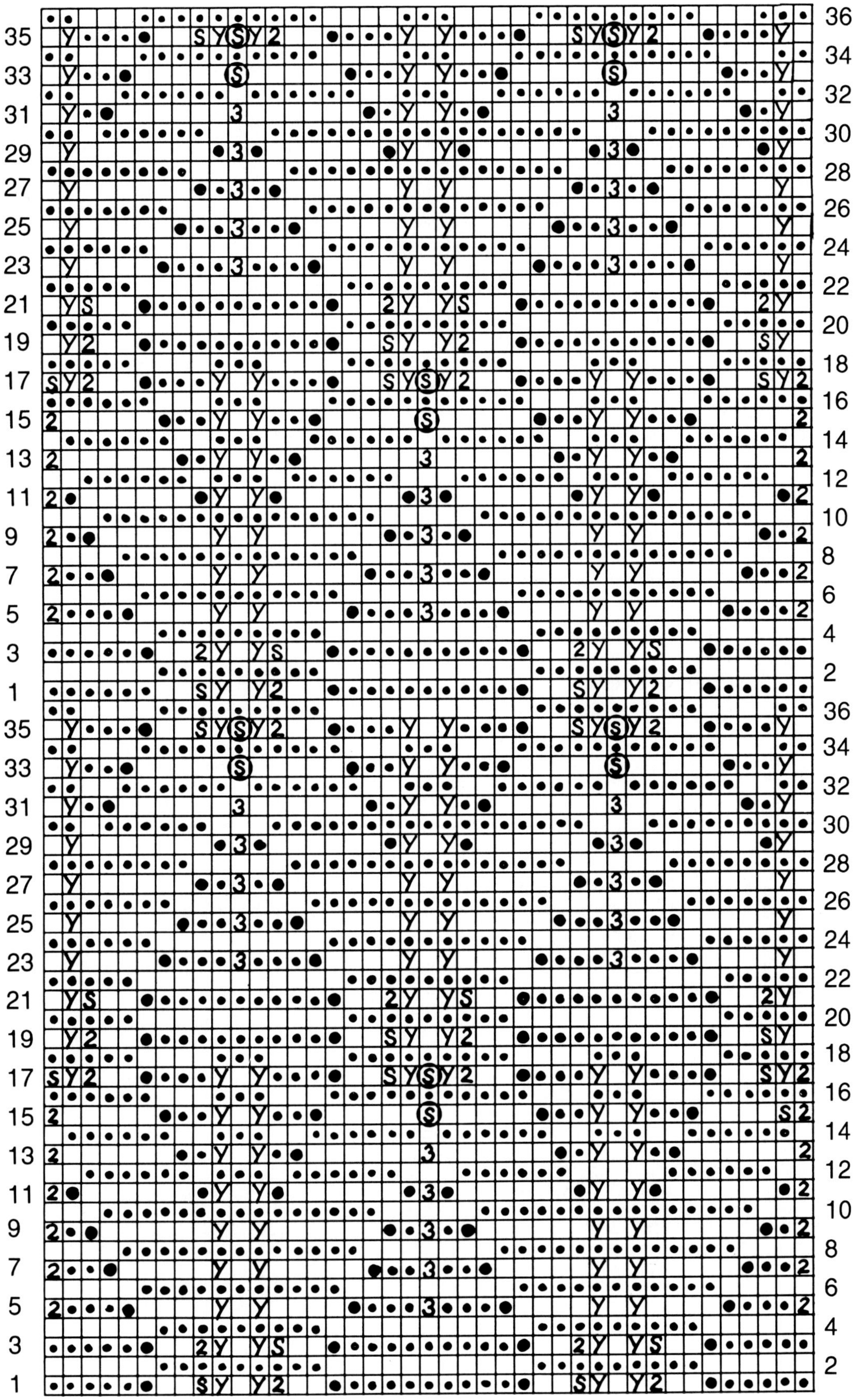

LACE LEAVES

PINK CLOUD
SWEATER
(Color photo page 51)

This ethereal sweater is at its luxurious best in a mist of pastel angora. If it is knitted in pure silk, cotton, or sport-weight wool, the pattern becomes clear and embossed, similar to needlepoint lace.

SIZE: Medium
This pattern has rather a lengthy repeat, and the size of the sweater can be changed easily only by adding a half or one whole leaf motif. Err on the large rather than the small side: Angora tends to shrink. Refer to the graph to increase or decrease a motif.

MATERIALS:
Yarn: Twenty-two 36-yard (33-meter) balls of 100% angora
or
sixteen 95-yard (89-meter) balls of angora and wool blend
or
pure silk, cotton, or sport-weight wool yarns

Needles: Straight knitting needles, U.S. sizes 3 and 6 (Continental sizes 3¼ and 4½)
Circular needles: 16 inches (40 centimeters) long, U.S. size 3 (Continental size 3¼)
Or sizes needed to obtain gauge
Notions: Row counter, stitch markers, tapestry needle

GAUGE: With larger needles, in pattern, 7 stitches = 1 inch (2.5 centimeters); 39 rows = 4 inches (10 centimeters)

FINISHED MEASUREMENTS:
Bust: 34 inches (86 centimeters)
Sleeve (measured at underarm seam): 20 inches (50.75 centimeters)
Length: 23 inches (58.5 centimeters)

Refer to page 89 for pattern stitch.

BACK
With smaller needles, cast on 111 sts and work k1, p1 ribbing for 1 inch (2.5 centimeters), ending with WS row. Change to larger needles and k, increasing 10 sts, evenly spaced, across row (RS) (121 sts). Commence pattern,

beginning with Row 1 (WS). Work 6 complete repeats of the 36-row pattern. Bind off all sts.

FRONT
Work same as for back.

SLEEVE
With smaller needles, cast on 50 sts and work k1, p1 ribbing for 1½ inches (3.75 centimeters). Change to larger needles and k, increasing to 101 sts (approximately 1 st in every st across). Again commence pattern, beginning on WS row, and work 5 complete leaf motifs.
Bind off all sts.
Work another sleeve in the same manner.

COLLAR
Sew shoulder seams, leaving 10 inches (25.5 centimeters) open at center. On circular needles, right sides facing, pick up 45 sts on front neck edge and 45 sts on back neck edge (90 sts). K every row for 1½ inches (3.75 centimeters) to make a small rolled collar. Bind off loosely.

FINISHING
Sew side seams. Sew underarm seams and set in sleeves.

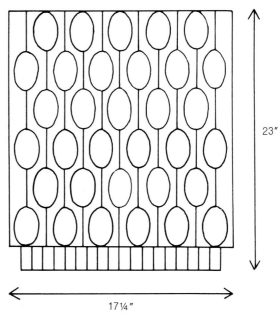

23″

17¼″

Front and Back

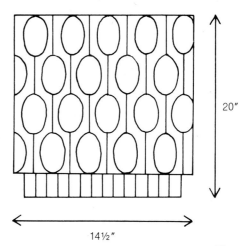

20″

14½″

Sleeve

HOW TO MAKE THE CASCADING WATERFALL PATTERN

This pattern is made by increasing and decreasing to form a wavy line. Its lacy effect is ideal for lightweight yarns with "loft," such as mohair and angora. The intricate-looking pattern is amazingly simple to do once you have mastered a few knitting basics.

Cascading waterfall—also known as *shell stitch, chevron stitch, feather stitch,* or *fan stitch*—may be executed in two ways. For the first, you increase by picking up and knitting the running thread between the stitches and decrease by purling two together. For the second method, you increase by taking the yarn over the needle to form an extra stitch and decrease by knitting two together.

Although the methods are similar, the first accentuates the wavy line; the second the holes in the pattern. Thus, the second method is more suitable for a fluffy yarn. Experiment: Knit a swatch each way to see which is most attractive with your yarn and garment.

The size of the scallop may be adjusted so long as you increase the same number of stitches you decrease.

CASCADING WATERFALL I
This pattern is worked on a multiple of 11 sts, plus 2 selvedge sts (see page 57).
ROW 1 (RS): Knit.
ROW 2: Purl.
ROW 3: *(P 2 tog) twice, (inc 1, k1) 3 times, inc 1, (p 2 tog) twice; repeat from * across row.

ROW 4: Purl.
Repeat from Row 1 for pattern.

CASCADING WATERFALL II
This pattern is worked on a multiple of 24 sts, plus 2 selvedge sts.
ROW 1: K 2 tog 4 times; *(yo, k1) 8 times, k 2 tog 8 times; repeat from *, ending last repeat k 2 tog 4 times.
ROW 2: K4, *p16, k8; repeat from *, ending last repeat k4.
ROWS 3 AND 5: Knit.
ROWS 4 AND 6: Purl.
Repeat from Row 1 for pattern.

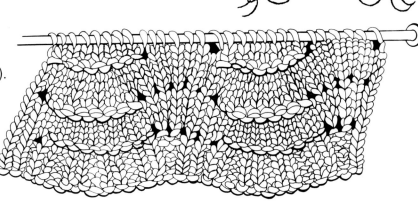

CASCADING WATERFALL SWEATER

(Color photo page 50)

Mohair in a dazzling color, a sweater shape of classic simplicity, and a soft-textured, lacy pattern all add up to a design with lasting appeal.

SIZES: Small [Medium]

MATERIALS:

Yarn: 10 [12] balls of Anny Blatt's Honey Moon Rouge (80% mohair, 20% silk)

Needles: Straight knitting needles, U.S. sizes 4 and 7 (Continental sizes 3¾ and 5). Circular needles, U.S. size 7 (Continental size 5)
Or sizes needed to obtain gauge

GAUGE: With larger needles, in pattern, 16½ stitches and 24 rows = 4 inches (10 centimeters)

FINISHED MEASUREMENTS:

Bust: 42½ inches (108 cm) [47 inches (119.5 cm)]

Sleeve (measured at underarm seam): 20 inches (50.75 centimeters) [20¾ inches (52.5 centimeters)]

Length: 24¼ inches (62.5 centimeters) [25 inches (63.5 centimeters)]

Refer to page 95 for pattern stitch I.

BACK

With smaller needles, cast on 90 [101] sts and work in k1, p1 ribbing for 1¾ inches (4.5 centimeters). Change to larger needles. Work evenly in cascading waterfall st, with 1 selvedge st at each side, until back measures 22¾ inches (58 centimeters) [23½ inches (60.5 centimeters)] overall.

Shape neck: Bind off center 18 [21] sts and finish each side of neck separately. Work 2 rows evenly, then bind off 6 sts at neck edge (30 [34] sts). Continue to work evenly in pattern. When back measures 24½ inches (61.5 cm) [25 inches (63.5 cm)], bind off remaining sts for shoulder.

Finish other side of neck, reversing shaping.

FRONT

Work same as for back until front

96

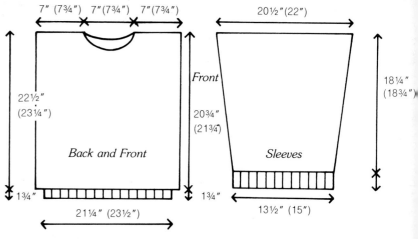

measures 20¾ inches (52.5 centimeters) [21¾ inches (55 centimeters)] overall.

Shape neck as for back. Work evenly in pattern until front measures same as back overall.

Bind off remaining 30 [34] sts for shoulder.

SLEEVE

With smaller needles, cast on 48 [54] sts and work in k1, p1 ribbing for 2 inches (5 centimeters).

Change to larger needles and work in cascading waterfall st. Inc 9 sts, evenly spaced, across first row (57 [63] sts). For size Small, start Row 3 as established. For size Medium, start Row 3 as follows: *K1, edge st, inc 1, (p 2 tog) 3 times, (inc 1, k1) 3 times, inc 1, and continue as established.

At the same time,

Shape sleeve: Inc 1 st at each side, alternating *every* 6th row once and *every* 8th row once, a total of 15 times (87 [93] sts). To keep in pattern, be sure to work same number of inside incs and decs. Continue to work evenly in pattern until sleeve measures 20 inches (50.75 centimeters) [20¾ inches (52.5 centimeters)] overall.

Bind off remaining sts.

Work another sleeve in the same manner.

FINISHING

Join shoulder seams.

Set sleeves in over 10¼ inches (26 centimeters) [11 inches (28 centimeters)] each side of shoulder seams.

Join side and sleeve seams.

Neckband: With circular needles, pick up 84 [90] sts, evenly spaced, around neck edge. Work k1, p1 ribbing in rounds, for 2 inches (5 centimeters).

Bind off loosely in ribbing.

CASCADING WATERFALL CAMISOLE
(Color photo page 50)

Because all you'll have to knit is the back and the front (no time-consuming sleeves!), you'll have this lovely camisole finished well in time for glamorous winter evenings. It is so light and off-the-shoulder that it can go on into spring, summer, and fall, too.

SIZES: Small [Medium]

MATERIALS:
Yarn: Ten 36-yard (33-meter) balls of angora, cashmere, or lambswool *or* any sport-weight yarn
Needles: Straight knitting needles, U.S. sizes 3 and 5 (Continental sizes 3¼ and 4)
Or sizes needed to obtain gauge

GAUGE: With larger needles, in pattern, 6 stitches = 1 inch (2.5 centimeters)

FINISHED MEASUREMENTS:

Bust: 30 inches (76 centimeters) [34 inches (86 centimeters)]

NOTE: The second method of doing the cascading waterfall pattern is recommended for this sweater and has been adapted below for size adjustments.

ROW 1 (RS): Small: (K2 tog) 4 times; *(yo, k1) 8 times; (k2 tog) 8 times; repeat from * twice, ending last repeat (k2 tog) 4 times.

Medium: (K2 tog) 5 times; *(yo, k1) 10 times; (k2 tog) 10 times; repeat from * twice, ending last repeat (k2 tog) 5 times.

ROW 2: Small: K4; *p16, k8; repeat from * twice, ending last repeat k4.

Medium: K5; *p20, k10; repeat from * twice, ending last repeat k5.

ROWS 3 AND 5: Knit.

ROWS 4 AND 6: Purl.

BACK

With smaller needles, cast on 88 [110] sts and work in k2, p2 ribbing for 1 inch (2.5 centimeters).

Change to larger needles. Work evenly in pattern until back measures 10 inches (25.5 centimeters) [11 inches (28 centimeters)] or desired length.

Work 4 rows St st.

Bind off.

FRONT

Work same as for back.

FINISHING

Sew side seams.

Single-crochet around the top of camisole for 2 rounds.

For straps, crochet a chain measuring approximately 14 inches (35.5 centimeters), or length desired. Work 1 row of sc into chain.

CASCADING WATERFALL COLLAR

This collar looks charming with the Classic Child's Dress (see page 78).

SIZE: One size fits all

MATERIALS:

Yarn: Sport weight

Needles: Straight knitting needles, U.S. size 5 (Continental size 4)
Or size needed to obtain gauge

GAUGE: In pattern, 11 stitches = 2 inches (5 centimeters)

Cast on 54 sts and knit 2 rows.

INC ROW: K twice into every stitch across row (108 sts). Proceed in pattern as follows:

ROW 1 (RS): Knit.

ROW 2: Purl.

ROW 3: *(K 2 tog) 3 times, (yo, k1) 6 times, (k 2 tog) 3 times; repeat from * across row.

ROW 4: Knit.

Repeat these 4 rows until collar measures approximately 2½ inches (6.25 centimeters) from cast-on edge. Bind off.

FINISHING

Sew collar to base of neckband.

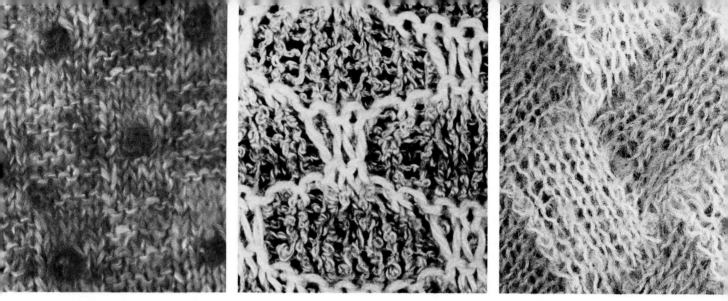

TEXTURE AND COLOR

Some patterns are naturals for color combinations. Diamond weave, for instance, done in four colors in the sweater on page 52, could also be done in many colors, with every diamond a sparkling contrast to the previous one. The mosaic effect of honeycomb stitch could be enhanced with different colors and shadings, framed with a single contrast color. Vertical bands of reverse stockinette stitch could be worked for a dolman-sleeved jacket, each band a different shade, from pale aqua through blue to lavender to light gray-brown. Or brilliant jewel colors could be contrasted in the basket weave stitch (shown on page 53) to heighten the effect of woven strips.

Join new colors at the beginning of the row so that the ends can be concealed in the seam later (see page 116). Experiment with all kinds of color changes and texture patterns.

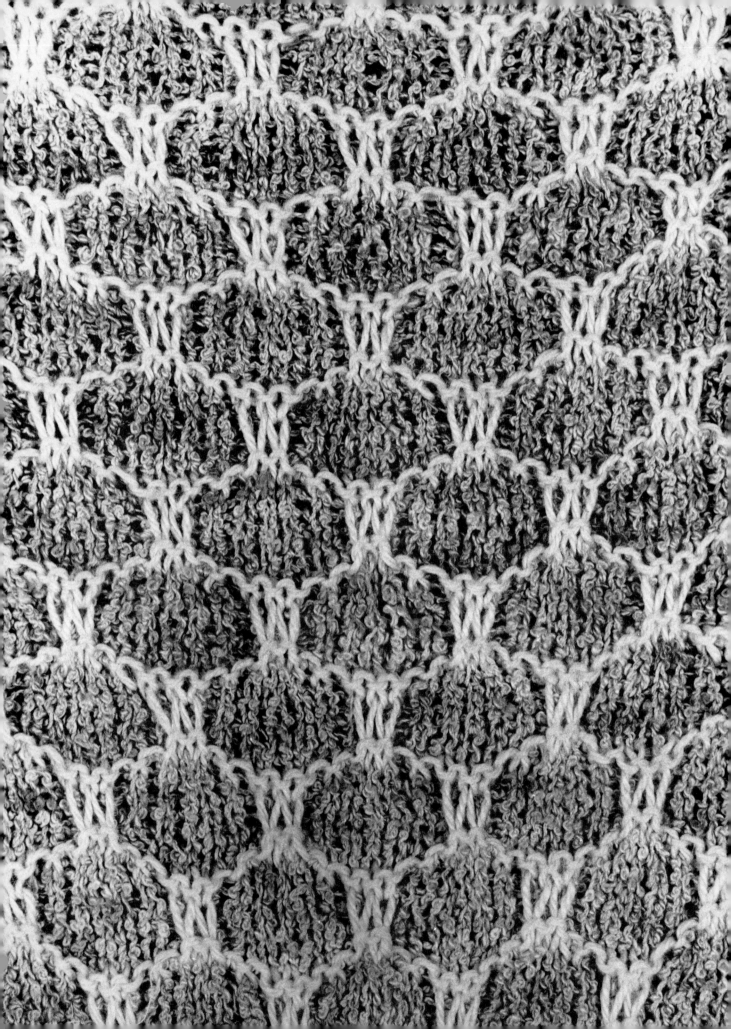

HOW TO MAKE
THE HONEYCOMB
HEXAGON PATTERN

Honeycomb patterns have a good deal of spring because of their construction. The contrast of texture shows well even if knitted in one color, but the honeycomb is accentuated if two colors are used.

Although it looks complex, the color change is simple. By slipping two stitches at intervals along the row, you carry the contrasting color over the main shade, which creates a waffle effect.

Using one color for the honeycomb outline, you could experiment with filling the centers with several different shades.

This pattern is worked on multiples of 8 sts plus 2 sts, plus 2 selvedge sts. Try the swatch in two colors.

ROWS 1 AND 2: In color A, knit.

ROWS 3, 5, AND 7: In color B, 1 selvedge st, k4; *sl 2 purlwise (yarn remains in back), k6; repeat from * across row, ending k4, 1 selvedge st.

ROWS 4, 6, AND 8: In color B, 1 selvedge st, p4; *sl 2 purlwise, p6; repeat from * across row, ending p4, 1 selvedge st.

ROWS 9 AND 10: In color A, knit.

ROWS 11, 13, AND 15: In color B, 1 selvedge st, *sl 2 purlwise (yarn remains in back), k6; repeat from * across row, ending sl 2 purlwise, 1 selvedge st.

ROWS 12, 14, AND 16: In color B, 1 selvedge st; *sl 2 purlwise, p6; repeat from * across row, ending sl 2 purlwise, 1 selvedge st.

Repeat from Row 1 for pattern.

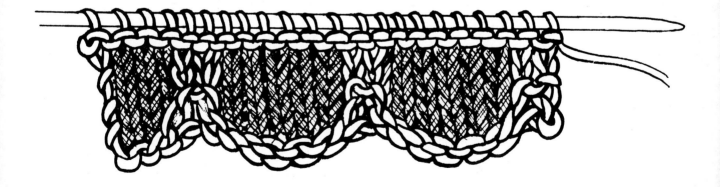

SILK HONEYCOMB PULLOVER

(Color photo page 48)

Knitted in handspun, hand-dyed silk, this sweater is luxuriously soft. This version has heather tones framed in natural ivory. Alternatively, it could be worked in contrasting fingering yarns—or in as many colors as a stained-glass window, with black as the outlining color.

SIZES: Small [Medium, Large]

MATERIALS:

Yarns: Approximately 1,200 yards (1,100 meters) *each* of *two* colors of Sheepish Grin pure silk *or* fingering yarns, mohair, or acrylic blends

Needles: Straight knitting needles, U.S. sizes 3 and 5
(Continental sizes 3¼ and 4)
Or sizes needed to obtain gauge

Notions: Stitch holders, tapestry needle

GAUGE: With larger needles, in pattern, 5 stitches and 8 rows = 1 inch (2.5 centimeters)

FINISHED MEASUREMENTS:

Bust: 37 inches (94 centimeters) [40 inches (101.5 centimeters), 43 inches (109.25 centimeters)]

Sleeve (measured at underarm seam): 18 inches (45.5 centimeters) [19 inches (48 centimeters), 19½ inches (49.5 centimeters)]

Length: 21 inches (53.5 centimeters) [22 inches (56 centimeters), 23 inches (58.5 centimeters)]

Refer to page 101 for pattern stitch.

BACK

With smaller needles and color A, cast on 82 [90, 98] sts and work k1, p1 ribbing for 3 inches (7.5 centimeters). On last row, inc 10 sts, evenly spaced, across row (92 [100, 108] sts). Change to larger needles.

Beginning with Row 3 of pattern, work evenly in pattern until back measures 20 inches (50.75 centimeters) [21 inches (53.5 centimeters), 22 inches (56 centimeters)], ending with last row of pattern.

Shape shoulders: Bind off 10 [11, 12] sts at beginning of next 6 rows (32 [34, 36] sts). Put sts on holder.

FRONT

Work same as for back until front measures about 17½ inches (44.5 centimeters) [18½ inches (47 centimeters), 19½ inches (49.5 centimeters)], ending with last row of pattern.

Shape neck: K38 [41, 43]. Place center 16 [18, 22] sts on holder. Join new balls of yarn and k remaining sts in row. Continue in pattern, working two sides separately. *At the same time,* on p side, p 2 tog at neck edge 4 [4, 3] times (34 [37, 40] sts each side). Continue working evenly in pattern until front measures 20 inches (50.75 centimeters) [21 inches (53.5 centimeters), 22 inches (56 centimeters)] overall.

Shape shoulders: Bind off 9 [10, 11] sts at beginning of next 3 rows, then 7 sts once for all sizes. Leave center sts on holder.

SLEEVE

With smaller needles and color A, cast on 38 [40, 44] sts and work k1, p1 ribbing for 2½ inches (6.25 centimeters). On last row, inc 14 [20, 24] sts, evenly spaced, across row (52 [60, 68] sts). Change to larger needles.

Beginning with Row 3 of pattern, work in pattern. *At the same time,* inc 1 st, each side, every inch (2.5 centimeters), until sleeve measures 18 inches (45.5 centimeters) [19 inches (48 centimeters), 19½ inches (49.5 centimeters)] overall. Bind off loosely.

Work another sleeve in the same manner.

FINISHING

For straight needles, sew 1 shoulder seam. For circular needles, sew both shoulder seams. Pick up 32 [34, 36] sts from holder at back neck, 17 [19, 20] sts at right neck, 16 [18, 22] sts from front neck, and 17 [19, 20] sts at left side (82 [90, 98] sts). Work k1, p1 ribbing for 5 rows.

Bind off loosely in ribbing.

Sew sleeve and side seams.

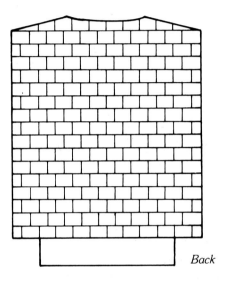

Back

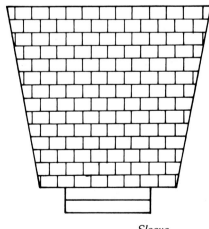

Sleeve

103

HOW TO MAKE THE DIAMOND WEAVE PATTERN

Diamond weave—also known as *woven lattice* and *entrelac*—is a fascinating design with its effect of ribbons interlaced diagonally. Although knitted in one piece, it appears to be separate bands woven together. It is effective in one color, with two contrasting colors, with softly blended shades, with many colors (every diamond a different color), or with contrasting textures (such as silk and angora). Some of the variations are illustrated on the facing page. The clever yet simple technique that gives this effect is done by first making a base row of triangles on the first row of knitting. On the next row, the spaces between the triangles are then filled with rectangles slanted to one side, diamond-fashion. The base of each of these rectangles is started by picking up the stitches along one side of each triangle. From then on, each successive row of strips consists of rectangles slanted in opposite directions. Finally, the spaces between the rectangles at the top of the piece are filled with another row of triangles. So that you can clearly understand the way

the stitch is worked, it is shown here and on page 106 on double-pointed needles. Once you realize that each separate row actually forms a continuous line of triangles or rectangles, you will find the pattern easy to work on a single set of straight needles (see page 107). To do this, begin by placing markers to separate each of the base triangles. As you develop the rhythm of working rectangles, you can eliminate the markers if you choose. Try a swatch in two colors with at least three base triangles so that you can see how the pattern develops.

This pattern is worked on a multiple of 6 sts. With color A, cast on 18 sts.

ROW 1 (BASE TRIANGLE ROW): *P 2 of cast-on sts, turn; k2, knitting into sts just purled, turn; p3, including 1 more of cast-on sts, turn; k3, knitting into sts just purled; repeat from * across row, working on 1 more of cast-on sts each p row until there are 6 purled sts on needle: 1 triangle made. *Do not turn.* Beg 2nd triangle by purling next 2 cast-on sts on needle. Repeat from * across row to make 2 more triangles. (See diagram.)

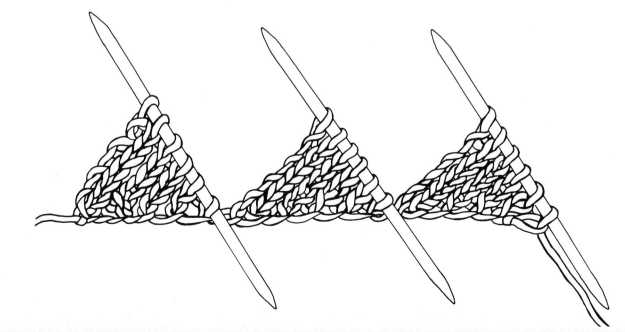

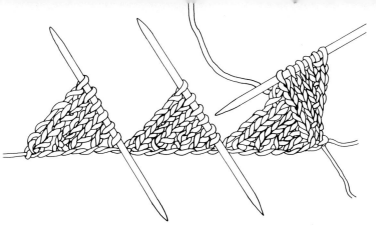

DIAMOND WEAVE

ROW 2 (RECTANGLE ROW): First half-rectangle at edge:

Attach color B. With RS facing, k2, turn; p2, turn; inc 1 st in 1st st by knitting into front and back of st, sl1, k1, psso, turn; p3, turn; inc 1 st in 1st st; k1, sl1, psso, turn; p4. Continue in same way, working 1 more st between the inc and the dec each time, until you have used up all sts in color A of the 1st base triangle and there are 6 color B sts on needle. Leave these sts on needle but do not fasten off yarn. (See diagram.)

Complete rectangles:

*Continuing to work with color B, pick up and k 6 sts along left edge of 1st base triangle (see diagram), turn; p these 6 sts, turn; k5; sl1, k1, psso (slipped st is last of 6 sts picked up and k st is 1st of following triangle), turn; p6, turn; k5; sl1, k1, psso, turn; p6. Continue to work in this manner until all color A sts have been worked. Repeat from * across row, picking up 6 sts along left edge of each of triangles following except last one.

Last half-rectangle:

Pick up and k 6 sts along left edge of last triangle, turn; p 2 tog, p4, turn; k5, turn; p 2 tog, p3, turn; k4, turn; continue until 1 st remains. Fasten off color B.

Diamond Weave Knitted on Double-Pointed Needles

106

NOTE: On subsequent repeats of row, sts will be picked up along *edge* of *rectangles* formed by previous row as opposed to base *triangles* referred to in instructions.

ROW 3: Attach color A. With remaining st still on right needle, turn and pick up and p 5 sts along straight edge of rectangle just completed, turn; *k6, turn; p5, p 2 tog, turn; continue in this manner until all color B sts have been worked. *Do not fasten off yarn.* Continue with color B to pick up and p 6 sts along side of following rectangle.

Repeat from * across row.

To form pattern, repeat Rows 2 and 3, so that rows of color blocks alternate.

TO BIND OFF: The top edge must be finished off by forming triangles to fill out the spaces formed by the last row of rectangles (which should be an RS row): Row 2.

From WS (1 st remaining on needle from previous row), pick up and p 5 sts along straight edge of triangle just completed, turn; *k6, turn; p 2 tog, p3, p 2 tog (1st of each color), k5, turn; p 2 tog, p2, p 2 tog, turn; k4, turn. Continue in this manner until 2 sts of each color remain. Then p1, p 2 tog (1 of each color), turn; k2, turn; p1, p 2 tog, sl 1st st over the p 2 tog: 1 st remains on needle.

Continue to bind off as necessary by forming triangles along previous row of rectangles; pick up and p 5 sts along side of following rectangle; repeat from * across row. Fasten off.

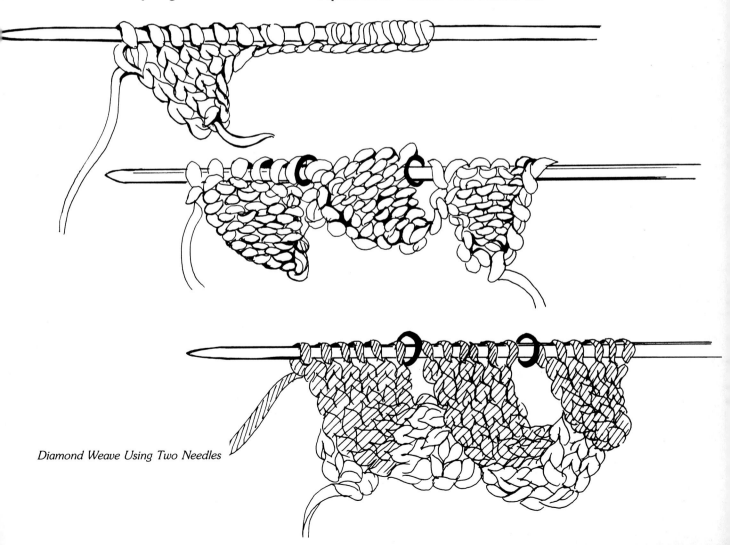

Diamond Weave Using Two Needles

DIAMOND WEAVE

DAZZLING DIAMOND WEAVE SWEATER
(Color photos page 52)

The sweater shown here was knitted in Lion Brand Molaine, a 100% acrylic yarn, in gray, peach, and natural. Page 52 shows the same diamond weave used for the whole sweater, in pink and gray. Use the instructions here for the body, and the White Cloud pattern on page 111 for the sleeve, knitting it long.

SIZES: Small [Medium, Large]

MATERIALS:
Yarn: 1.4-ounce (40-gram) balls of Lion Brand Molaine
    8 balls of gray *(A)*
    2 balls of peach *(B)*
        plus
    Two 1.4-ounce (40-gram) balls of natural *(C)* Lion Brand Wollana
        or
    Sport-weight mohair or wool
Needles: Straight double-pointed knitting needles, U.S. size 8 (Continental size 5½)
Or size needed to obtain gauge

GAUGE: In stockinette stitch, 4 stitches = 1 inch (2.5 centimeters)

FINISHED MEASUREMENTS:
Bust: 37 inches (94 centimeters) [40 inches (101.5 centimeters), 42½ inches (108 centimeters)]
Sleeve (measured at underarm seam): 20 inches (50.75 centimeters)
Length: 24 inches (61 centimeters)

FRONT
With smaller needles and color A, cast on 74 [80, 86] sts and work k2, p2 ribbing for 3 inches (7.5 centimeters). On RS, dec 32 sts evenly across last row of ribbing (42 [48, 54] sts). With larger needles, begin to work diamond weave pattern (page 105) over remaining sts, forming a base row of 7 [8, 9] triangles, each worked over 6 sts, in color A. Repeat Rows 2 and 3 so that rows of color blocks continue to fall in following sequence: *A, B, A, C; repeat from * (so that Row 3 is always color A, and color B alternates with color C for Row 2). Continue to work evenly in pattern, following chart on page 109 for correct size.

Shape armholes: From WS (1 st remaining on needle from previous row), pick up and p 5 sts along straight edge of triangle just completed, turn; *k6, turn; p 2 tog, p3, p 2 tog (1 st of each color), k5, turn; p 2 tog, p2, p 2 tog, turn; k4, turn; repeat from * until 2 sts of each color remain. Then p1, p 2 tog (1 of each color), turn; k2, turn; p1, p 2 tog, sl st over the p 2 tog; 1 st remains on needle; repeat from * across row, forming color A rectangles. To form last triangle, pick up and p 6 sts along straight edge of color B rectangle in row below. Repeat from * until 1 st remains on needle.
Fasten off.

BACK

Cast on 74 [80, 86] sts and work k2, p2 ribbing for 3 inches (7.5 centimeters). Work evenly in St st until back measures same as front to underarm.

Shape armholes: Bind off 9 [10, 11] sts at beginning of next 2 rows (56 [60, 64] sts). Continue to work evenly on remaining sts until back measures same as front from armhole shaping—approximately 7½ inches (19 centimeters).

Shape shoulders: Bind off 3 [4, 5] sts at beginning of next 4 rows.
Bind off 4 sts at beginning of next 6 rows (20 sts). Place remaining sts on holder.

SLEEVE

Cast on 46 sts and work k2, p2 ribbing for 3 inches (7.5 centimeters). Then work St st. *At the same time,* inc 1 st, each side, every 4 rows, 12 times (70 sts). Work evenly in St st until sleeve measures 14 inches (35.5 centimeters). Inc 1 st, each side, every 4 rows, 4 times (78 sts). Continue to work evenly until sleeve measures 18 inches (45.5 centimeters) or desired length to underarm.

Cast on 4 sts at beginning of next 2 rows (86 sts). Continue to work evenly for 2½ inches (6.25 centimeters) more. Bind off 30 sts at beginning of next 2 rows (26 sts). Continue to work evenly for 4½ inches (11.5 centimeters) [5 inches (12.5 centimeters), 5½ inches (14 centimeters)]. Place remaining 26 sts on holder.
Work another sleeve in same manner.

FINISHING

Sew front and back to sleeve and shoulder sections. Sew sleeve and side seams. To finish neck, on double-pointed needles, work sts from holders and pick up on front as follows: Starting at left back shoulder seam, k on 26 sts from holder, dec 6 sts evenly spaced; pick up 12 sts across front; k on 26 sts from holder on other sleeve, dec 6 sts evenly spaced, k 20 sts from back holder, join and work in rounds of k2, p2 rib on 72 sts for 2 inches. Bind off loosely. Turn to inside and sew in place.

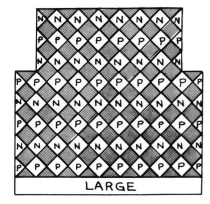

LARGE

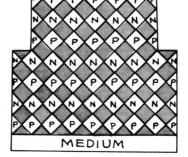

MEDIUM

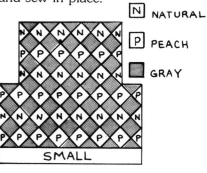

SMALL

N NATURAL
P PEACH
GRAY

109

WHITE CLOUD EVENING SWEATER
(Color photo page 53)

The diamond weave pattern in silky ribbon and angora used for the sleeves of a surplice-back sweater makes an interesting and subtle effect. You can try combining cotton and mohair, or a bouclé with a smooth yarn, all in the same shades.

This sweater is low and backless. If the back is made the same as the front, a boat-neck design will be the result.

SIZES: Small [Medium, Large]

MATERIALS:
Yarn: Ten 77-yard (70.5-meter) spools of ⅛-inch (.2-centimeter) wide Knitting Fever Dorothé Bis Borneo ribbon (100% viscose)
or Look'Anny, Crystal Palace Mikado, *or* Pingouin ribbon
plus
6 balls of single-ply angora
Needles: Straight knitting needles, U.S. sizes 7 and 10 (Continental sizes 5 and 6½)
Or sizes needed to obtain gauge
Notions: Tapestry needle, sewing thread, sewing needle

GAUGE: With larger needles, in stockinette stitch, 7 stitches = 2 inches (5 centimeters); 11 rows = 2 inches (5 centimeters)

FINISHED MEASUREMENTS:
Bust: 32 inches (81 cm) [34 inches (86 cm), 36 inches (91.5 cm)]
Sleeve (measured at underarm seam): 11 inches (28 centimeters)
Length: 19 inches (48 centimeters)
Refer to page 105 for pattern stitch.

RIGHT BACK
With smaller needles, cast on 64 [68, 72] sts and work k1, p1 ribbing for 3½ inches (9 centimeters). Change to larger needles and continue in St st. *At the same time,* at left edge of back, dec 1 st every row, 32 times, then 1 st every other row 12 [14, 16] times (20 [22, 24] sts). When right back measures 11 inches (28 centimeters) overall,
    Shape armholes: Bind off 4 sts at beginning of next 2 rows. Dec 1 st, each side, next 4 RS rows (48 [52,

sts). Work evenly in St st for 7 inches (17.75 centimeters) [7½ inches (18.75 centimeters), 8 inches (20 centimeters)] more.
Bind off all sts.

LEFT BACK
Pick up 64 [68, 72] sts at top of ribbing behind right back (work in same stitches so that right back and left back are attached).
Work same as for right back, reversing shaping.

FRONT
With smaller needles, cast on 64 [68, 72] sts and work k1, p1 ribbing for 3½ inches (9 centimeters).
Change to larger needles and continue to work evenly in St st until front measures 11 inches (28 centimeters) overall.

    Shape armholes: Bind off 4 sts at beginning of next 2 rows. Dec 1 st, each side, next 4 RS rows (48 [52,

56] sts). Continue to work evenly for 7 inches (17.75 centimeters) [7½ inches (19 centimeters), 8 inches (20 centimeters)] more.
Bind off remaining sts.

SLEEVE
With smaller needles, cast on 42 sts and work k1, p1 ribbing for 2½ inches (6.25 centimeters). On last row, inc 6 sts, evenly spaced, across row (48 sts). Change to larger needles. Work diamond weave pattern in repeats of 8 sts each diamond, working alternate rows of silk and angora, as shown below, until chart is complete.
Bind off on triangle row with silk.
Work another sleeve in the same manner.

FINISHING
Sew side seams. Sew sleeves into armholes, forming a pleat at the top.
Work 1 row sc with angora all around neckline.

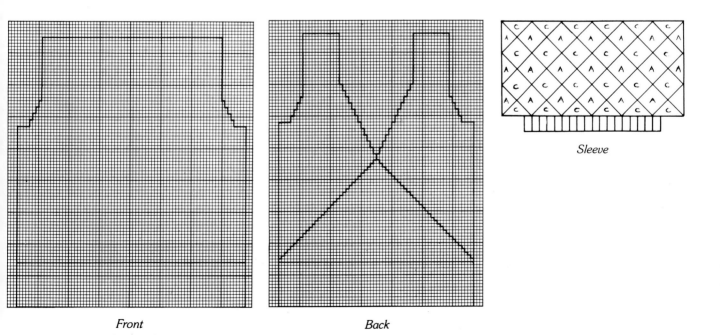

Front

Back

Sleeve

HOW TO MAKE BOBBLES AND BANDS

To make a simple basket weave, you can work garter-stitch rectangles and stockinette-stitch rectangles alternately on multiples of, for instance, 10 stitches. After a little experimentation, however, you will discover that simply to work 5 garter stitches and 5 stockinette stitches for 5 rows and then alternate the blocks tends to look untidy. If you separate the blocks by working 1 row of knit and 1 of purl on every 6th and 7th row, an attractive woven effect will result.

To accentuate the overlapping of the stockinette stitch and make a real basket weave, you can work as follows:

BASKET WEAVE PATTERN
This pattern is worked on a multiple of 10 sts.

ROWS 1 AND 7: Knit.

ROWS 2 AND 8: Purl.

ROWS 3 AND 5: *K2, p6, k2; repeat from * across row.

ROWS 4 AND 6: *P2, k6, p2; repeat from * across row.

ROWS 9 AND 11: *P3, k4, p3; repeat from * across row.

ROWS 10 AND 12: *K3, p4, k3; * repeat from * across row.

Repeat from Row 1 to form pattern.

Bobbles—attractive raised, rounded knobs—can be made in different sizes, but they are all made on the same principle: by working a cluster of 4 or 5 stitches into 1 stitch and then working 4 or more rows of stockinette stitch into these same stitches. Bobbles—also called *popcorns*—in self-color (matching their background) can be very effective when combined with textures such as cables. But bobbles may also be worked in many colors, like scattered confetti over a plain stockinette-stitch ground. Alternatively, try working them in a single contrast color on a basket weave pattern, as shown in the sweater on page 46.

BOBBLES
Each bobble is made by working a cluster of 5 sts into 1 st and working 4 rows of St st (k 1 row, p 1 row) over these 4 sts.

ROW 1 (RS): K2; place marker on needle. *Drop color A yarn and tie on a length of color B yarn. In next st, using color B, k, p, k, p, k (5 sts worked in 1 st). Turn work, p all 5 sts, turn, k all 5 sts, turn, p all 5 sts, turn, k all 5 sts; do not turn work. With left needle, pass the first 4 sts, one after the other, over the 5th st, which remains on the needle: 1 bobble made. Drop the end of color B yarn; do not cut. Pick up color A yarn, continue in pattern, repeating bobbles as needed.

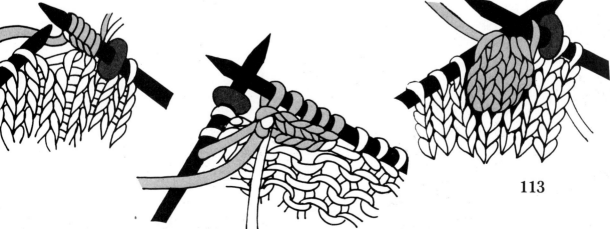

113

BOBBLES AND BANDS JACKET
(Color photo page 46)

The flattering line of soft, rounded shoulders is accentuated in this jacket by horizontal stripes that run right across the tops of the sleeves. Muted tones of mohair combined with silky yarn give this oversized, hip-length jacket a luxurious softness, and the fluffy texture makes the basket weave mesh softly. The sleeves are long, but are designed to be worn pushed up.

SIZE: One size fits all

MATERIALS:

Yarn: 1¾-ounce (50-gram) balls of Anny Blatt's Bright'Anny (52% mohair, 35% viscose, 13% acrylic)
    13 balls of Gris (gray) *(A)*
    3 balls of Acier (steel gray) *(B)*
    3 balls of Tulipe (burgundy) *(C)*

Needles: Straight knitting needles, U.S. sizes 7 and 10 (Continental sizes 5 and 6½)
Or sizes needed to obtain gauge

Notions: Stitch holders, 6 buttons, tapestry needle

GAUGE: With larger needles, in basket weave stitch, 13 stitches and 20 rows = 4 inches (10 centimeters)

FINISHED MEASUREMENTS:
Bust: 48 inches (122 centimeters)
Sleeve (measured at underarm seam): 19 inches (48 centimeters)
Length: 25 inches (63.5 centimeters)

Refer to page 113 for pattern stitch.

BACK
With smaller needles and color B, cast on 70 sts and work k1, p1 ribbing for 3½ inches (9 centimeters).
Change to larger needles and color A for basket weave, color C for bobbles. Work in basket weave, increasing 10 sts, evenly spaced, across the 1st row (80 sts). Work evenly in pattern until back measures 17 inches (43 centimeters).
    Shape armholes: Bind off each side, every other row, 3 sts once and 1 st twice (70 sts). Then continue in garter st, as follows: *2 rows (1 garter rib) with color C, 2 rows with color A. Repeat from * for striped pattern. When back measures 25 inches (63.5 centimeters) overall, bind off all remaining sts.

RIGHT FRONT

With smaller needles and color B, cast on 40 sts and work k1, p1 ribbing for 3½ inches (9 centimeters).

Change to larger needles and color A, and work evenly in basket weave until front measures 17 inches (43 centimeters).

Shape armholes: Bind off at left side, every other row, 3 sts once and 1 st twice (35 sts). Continue evenly in striped garter st as for back until front measures 21½ inches (54.5 centimeters).

Shape neck: Bind off, at right side, every other row: 10 sts once, 2 sts 3 times, and 1 st once (18 sts). When front measures 25 inches (63.5 centimeters) overall, bind off remaining sts for shoulder.

LEFT FRONT

Work same as for right front, reversing shaping.

SLEEVE

With smaller needles and color B, cast on 35 sts and work k1, p1 ribbing for 2 inches (5 centimeters).

Change to larger needles and color A. Work in basket weave, increasing 10 sts, evenly spaced, across 1st row (45 sts).

Shape sleeves: Inc 1 st each side every 10th row, 6 times (57 sts), until sleeve measures 13¾ inches (35 centimeters) overall.

Shape cap: Bind off, each side, every other row: 2 sts twice, 1 st 12 times, and 2 sts twice (17 sts). *At the same time,* when sleeve measures 17 inches (43 centimeters), continue in striped garter st, as for back.

Bind off remaining sts after completing side decreases.

Work another sleeve in the same manner.

FRONT BORDERS

With smaller needles and color B, cast on 5 sts and work k1, p1 ribbing. When border measures ¾ inch (2 centimeters), make buttonhole of 1 st (work 2 sts tog, yo) over center st. Make 4 more buttonholes in the same manner, spacing them 3¼ inches (8.25 centimeters) apart. When border measures 21¼ inches (54 centimeters), put border sts on holder. Work a second border, omitting buttonholes.

FINISHING

Join shoulder seams. Set sleeves in. Join side and sleeve seams. Sew front borders to corresponding right and left fronts.

Neck border: With smaller needles, pick up 81 sts, evenly spaced, around neck edge (including sts on holders for right and left front borders). Work k1, p1 ribbing. On the 1st row, form 1 buttonhole in line with buttonholes on front border.

When neck border measures 1½ inches (3.75 centimeters), bind off in ribbing. Fold neck border in half to outside and sl st in place.

Sew buttons opposite buttonholes.

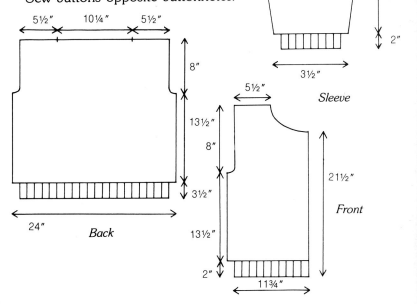

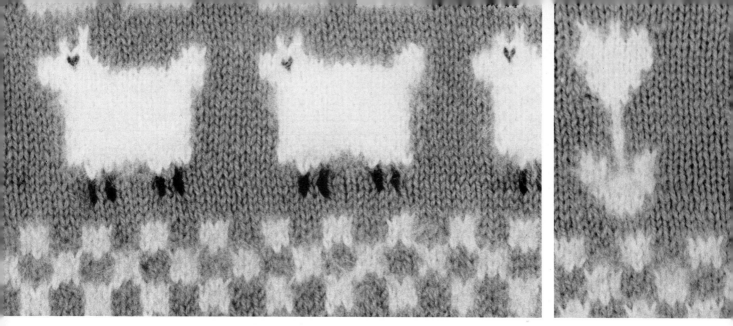

CHANGING COLORS

Once you learn the comparatively simple process of color changing, your sweaters can blossom into a garden of color. Any pattern—abstract, realistic, all-over repeat, bold or miniature in scale, textured or smooth—can be worked out by following a graph, changing color by one of the following methods.

The simplest color change is the horizontal stripe, for which the pattern follows the stitch. You join each new color at the beginning of the row, where ends can be buried in the seam, and work with even bands or stripes of varying widths. If you join each new color on the right side, or face, there will be a clean line where the colors join. If you join on the wrong (reverse) side, a separate thin stripe of the new color is formed at the join. If you wish, you can deliberately make this stripe a pattern feature by alternating bands of stockinette stitch, always joining the new color on the purl side.

A second simple color-change pattern is vertical stripes. To knit these, you must join on a new ball of yarn at every color change along the row. If you have four blue vertical stripes on a white ground, for instance, you must join on eight balls of yarn, a separate ball for each color change. Because so many balls of yarn are apt to become tangled, bobbins are used for this kind of pattern (see page 125).

Bobbins are also used for any pattern with large isolated areas, such as the hearts in the Sheep and Hearts Sweater on page 45. But for smaller repeats, such as the checkerboard stripe in the same pattern, you must carry the yarn across the back; it would be impossible to have a bobbin for each one. The threads—"floats"—that lie at the back would catch if stretched too far from one point to another. Therefore, they are woven in. This method, called stranding or weaving, is ideal for colors that repeat frequently across the row. It is difficult to work with more than three colors in a row at one time, one being worked while the others are being stranded or carried. But you can increase the apparent number by following the horizontal-stripe technique just described, making alternating rows of color,

116

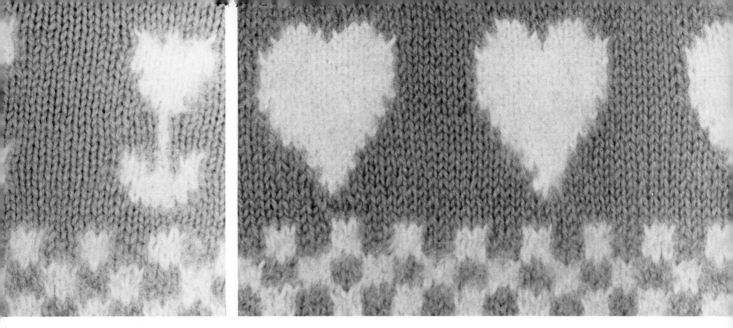

and by picking up stitches (by slip stitch) from the previous row, just as in the honeycomb-stitch method (see page 101). This can produce intricate-looking patterns similar to those from Shetland and the Fair Isles.

If you further expand color changing with duplicate stitch and embroidery, the sky's the limit! Plaids can be easily made, for instance, by knitting horizontal bands of color and repeating the same colors vertically in duplicate stitch (see page 147).

To design patterns of your own, work with the knitter's graph paper on page 176, trying out different color schemes in crayon. The selection of patterns that follows is to give you ideas. You can work them with bobbins, with stranding or weaving, with duplicate stitch, or with a combination of these methods.

Intarsia knitting, forming patterns in several colors, is one of the oldest—and today, conversely, one of the newest—ways of designing a sweater. *Intarsia* is a term that originated in the Renaissance to describe the art or technique of making inlaid designs, especially in woodwork or mosaics. In knitting, the original meaning of *intarsia* is to add detail to a pattern by transferring a block of stitches to smaller needles, increasing the number of stitches and rows, and working the section separately. With more stitches in a particular area, greater detail could be added. Today, the word *intarsia* has almost become a generic term meaning any kind of knitting done in more than one color to resemble jacquard repeat patterns. It can also be thought of as motif- or picture-knitting. As well as being one of the oldest knitting concepts, intarsia is one of the most sophisticated.

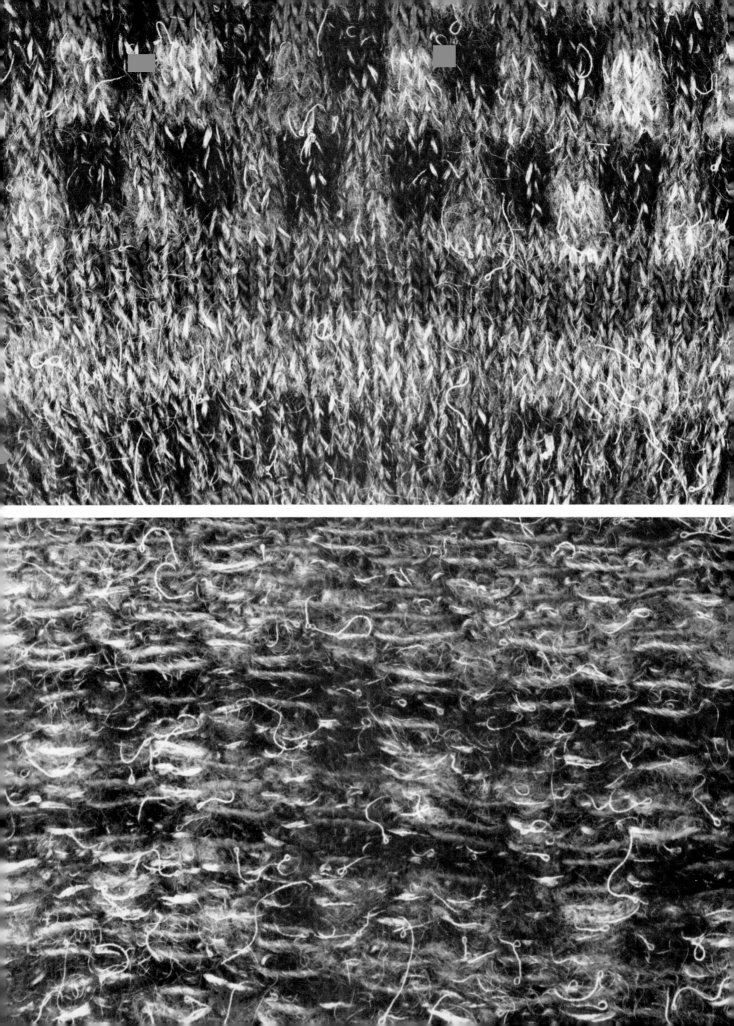

CHANGING COLORS USING WEAVING

If there are a great many colors alternating in one row, weaving and carrying the yarn will be the most suitable way of changing colors. Especially for smaller repeats, such as the checkerboard stripe in the same pattern, you must carry the yarn across the back; it would be impossible to have a bobbin for each one. Also, the threads that lie at the back—floats—would catch if stretched too far from one point to another. Therefore, they are woven in. This method, called *stranding* or *weaving,* is ideal when a few colors are repeated frequently across the row.

Knitting: Light yarn below needle. The light thread is being carried. The dark thread is being knitted; therefore, it stays in the right hand while the light color stays in the left. The light (carried) color is held alternately above and below the needle. The arrow shows how the dark thread will wrap around the needle to form a knit stitch. The light thread will fall off the needle as the stitch is taken, but will be locked in the dark thread.

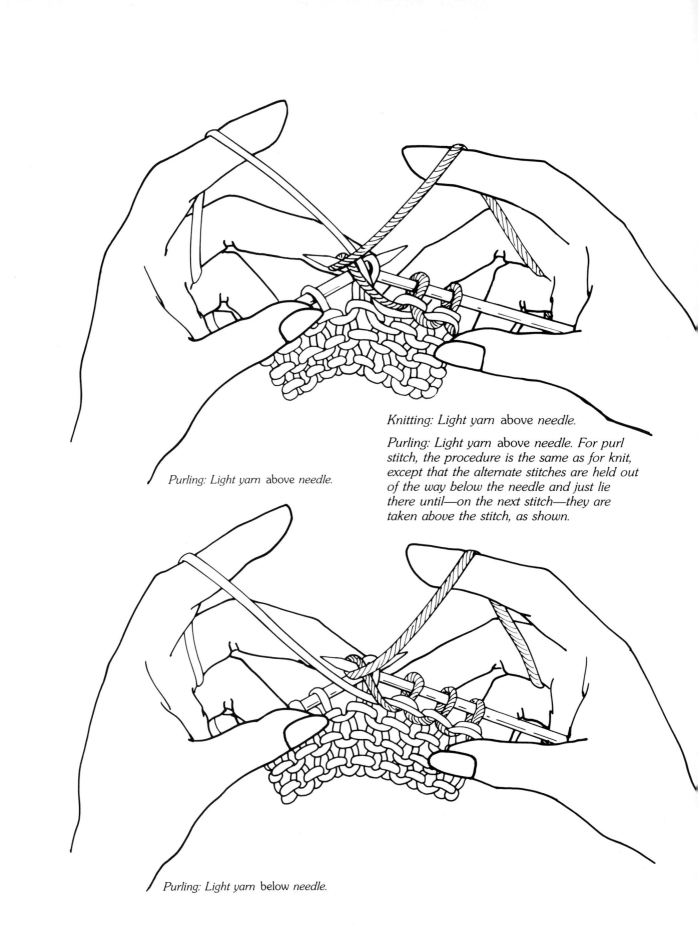

Knitting: *Light yarn* above *needle.*

Purling: *Light yarn* above *needle.* For purl stitch, the procedure is the same as for knit, except that the alternate stitches are held out of the way below the needle and just lie there until—on the next stitch—they are taken above the stitch, as shown.

Purling: *Light yarn* above *needle.*

Purling: *Light yarn* below *needle.*

CONTEMPORARY FAIR ISLE PULLOVER

(Color photo page 46)

Starblitz, or "shooting stars," is an apt name for the variegated yarn used for this oversized pullover, which has subtle glints of silver-gray all through it. Because the wools are blended, the overall effect is misty and soft; there are no strong contrasts.

SIZE: One size fits all

MATERIALS:
Yarn: Six 1¾-ounce (50-gram), 135-yard (125-meter) balls of Anny Blatt's Starblitz (mohair, polyamide blend) Mars (dark gray with silver glint) *(main color)*
    plus
1⅖-ounce (40-gram) 75-yard (60-meter) balls of Silk'Anny (100% silk)
 1 ball of Prune (dark purple-red) *(A)*
 1 ball of Chataigne (chestnut brown) *(D)*

    plus
1¾-ounce (50-gram), 60-yard (55-meter) balls of Laser (mohair blend)
 1 ball of Chataigne (chestnut brown) *(B)*
 2 balls of Noir (black) *(C)*
Needles: Straight knitting needles, U.S. sizes 4, 8, and 10½ (Continental sizes 3½, 5½, and 7)
Or sizes needed to obtain gauge

GAUGE: With largest needles, in stockinette stitch jacquard, 17 stitches and 24 rows = 4 inches (10 centimeters)
With medium needles, 16 stitches and 22 rows = 4 inches (10 centimeters)

FINISHED MEASUREMENTS:
Bust: 43½ inches (110.5 centimeters)
Sleeve (measured at underarm seam): 20 inches (50.75 centimeters)
Length: 26½ inches (67.25 centimeters)

For jacquard pattern, follow chart, using the weaving technique for changing colors, page 119.

BACK

With smaller needles and main color, cast on 92 sts and work k1, p1 ribbing for 4½ inches (11.5 centimeters). Change to largest needles and begin St st jacquard, following chart. Work evenly until back measures 15¾ inches (40 centimeters) overall.

Shape armholes: Bind off, each side, every other row, 2 sts twice and 1 st 3 times (78 sts). After completing chart, change to medium needles and main color, and work St st.

Inc 1 st, each side, when back measures 23½ inches (60.5 centimeters) overall. Work even until back measures 26½ inches (67.25 centimeters) overall.

Shape shoulders: Bind off 12 sts at beginning of row; k 12 sts; bind off center 32 sts; k 24 sts.

Next row: Bind off 12 sts at beginning of row; p12, turn; k 1 row, turn; bind off remaining sts. Work other side in same manner, reversing shaping.

FRONT

Work as for back until front measures 23½ inches (60.5 centimeters) overall.

Shape neck: Bind off center 10 sts and continue each side separately, binding off at neck edge, every other row, 4 sts once, 2 sts twice, and 1 st 3 times.

When front measures 26½ inches (67.25 centimeters) overall,

Shape shoulders as for back. Work other side the same way, reversing shaping.

SLEEVE

With smallest needles and main color, cast on 50 sts and work k1, p1 ribbing for 2¾ inches (7 centimeters). Change to medium needles and St st. Inc, each side, every 4th row, 3 sts in

from edge, 1 st 20 times (90 sts). Work in pattern until sleeve measures 15¾ inches (40 centimeters) overall.

Shape cap: Bind off, each side, every other row, 3 sts 7 times, 6 sts twice (24 sts). Bind off remaining stitches.

FINISHING

Sew right shoulder seam.

Neckband: With smallest needles, pick up 101 sts, evenly spaced, around neck edge. With main color, work k1, p1 ribbing for ¾ inch (2 centimeters). Bind off in ribbing.

Sew left shoulder and neckband seam. Set sleeves in.

Join side and sleeve seams.

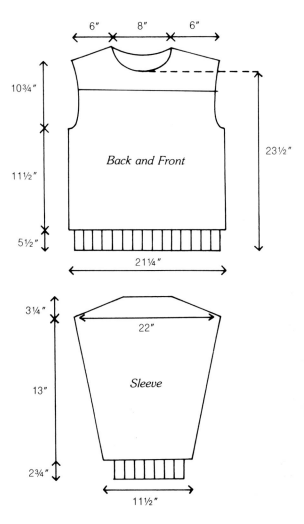

122

Key

Starblitz
dark gray

Chataigne
Chestnut brown

Silk
Chataigne

Silk prune

Laser
noir (black)

To knit pattern, turn chart so that the long measurement becomes horizontal.

123

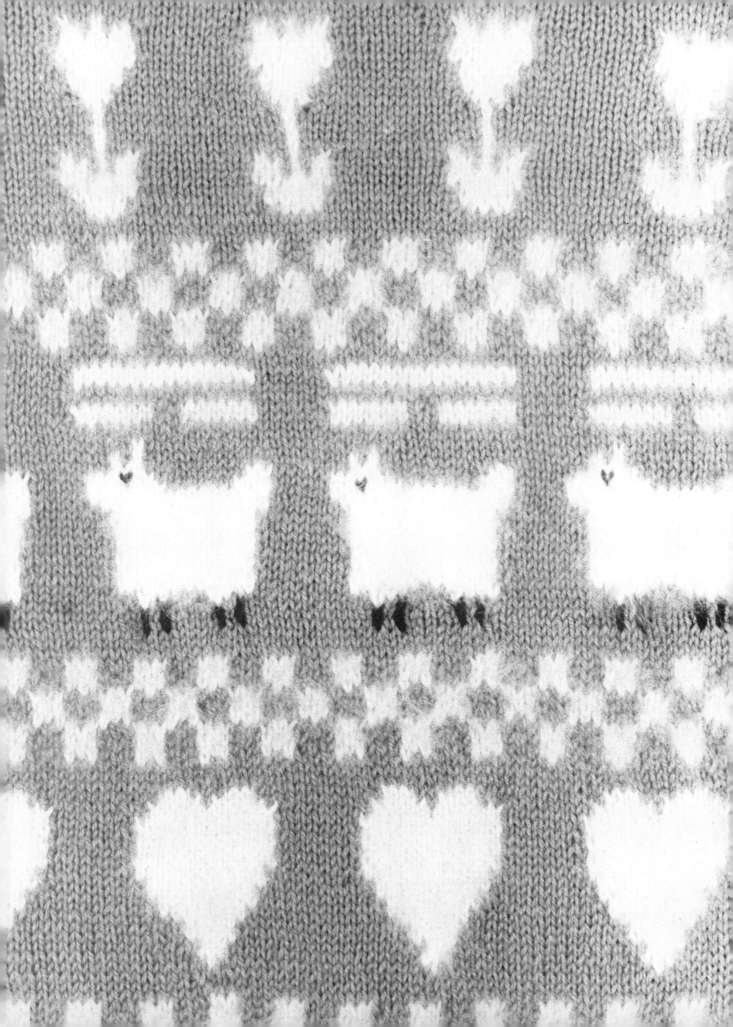

HOW TO CHANGE COLORS USING BOBBINS

Determine first whether your pattern is more suitable for bobbins or for weaving. The number of stitches in each color in each row is the deciding factor. The bobbin method is best for repeat patterns with relatively few color changes. First, count the number of times the colors change along the row. For every color change, you will need a bobbin. The bobbin is an ingenious little device that holds small amounts of yarn. It is indispensable to prevent tangling. A guard at the end with a diagonal slit allows you to wind the yarn easily, but holds it so that it cannot unwind as you knit. This allows you to regulate the length of yarn you unwind as the bobbin hangs from your knitting. The shorter lengths do not twist or tangle as often as do the long strands from unwinding balls of yarn.

Wind the bobbins with the required colors and begin knitting. Join each new color on the face, or knit, row to keep a clean line. As each color change occurs along the row, twist the new color to be used once around the old (see diagram). This prevents openings from forming in the knitting where the colors join. To prevent tangling, unwind just enough yarn to knit easily (two complete twists).

Right side: The color changes 5 times along the row, so there is a bobbin for each color. *Illustration continued on page 126.*

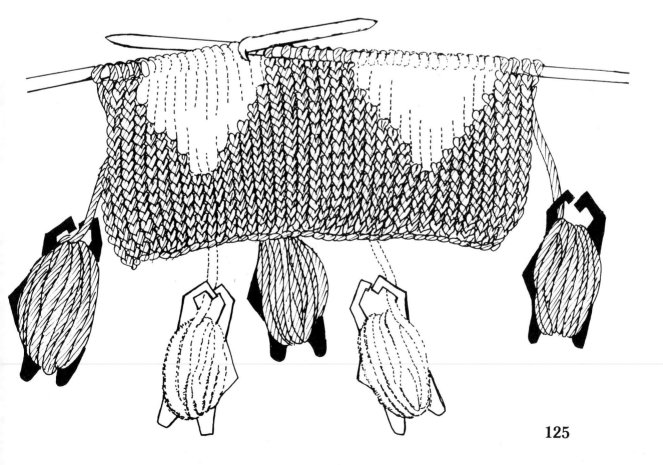

CHANGING BOBBINS

In order to reproduce intarsia patterns accurately, you must follow a graph. On the square grid, each square represents a stitch, and symbols show which colors to use. Some knitters prefer to enlarge graphs on a photocopier and fill in the correct colors with crayons before beginning to knit.

Start following graphs from the lower right corner. If you are using straight needles, work from right to left for your facing or knit row, and then work back on the purl row from left to right. Continue switching from right-to-left to left-to-right as you work upward. If you use circular needles, begin each row on the right.

A magnetized strip on a metal board is a useful gadget: You move the strip up row by row as you work, so that you can keep your place easily. In case you are interrupted halfway along a row, always keep a pencil handy to mark the place where you left off.

A chart of perfect squares does not give a true representation of knitted stitches, which are always broader than they are tall. "Squares" on knitter's graph paper are actually rectangular to give a better idea of the real proportions of the stitches. When following designs from square graphs, remember that the knitted pattern will be slightly broader than it appears on the graph. Knitter's graph paper is provided on page 176 so that you can try graphing designs of your own.

Wrong (reverse) side: This shows the knitting in process as seen from the back. Before picking up the pink bobbin to knit, twist it once around the blue bobbin. This prevents a hole from forming where the two colors join. The place on each row where this twisting occurs shows as a broken line around the heart. You can also combine bobbins with the weaving technique described on page 119. Both methods are excellent for knitting in several colors, following graphs of needlepoint designs, or adapting the pattern from the fabric of a skirt—to make a matching sweater, for instance. Knitter's graph paper is very useful for this (see page 176).

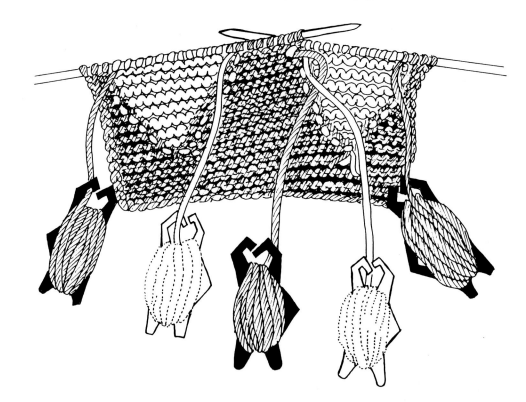

SHEEP AND HEARTS SWEATER

(Color photos pages 44–45)

Combining fluffy angora with flat-textured knitting worsted or cotton is an interesting way to bring out the character of this pattern, though it is equally attractive knitted in a mohair blend, brushed to give an all-over softness.

SIZES: Small [Medium, Large]

MATERIALS:
Yarn: Ten 1¾-ounce (50-gram), 145-yard (132.5-meter) balls of Chat Botté's Petrouchka

or

Eight 1⅖-ounce (40-gram) balls of Lion Brand Molaine

plus

100% angora
    2 balls *each* of aqua and pink
    1 ball of white
    1 ball (or scraps) of black

or

Lion Brand Molaine, 1 ball of each color

Needles: Straight knitting needles, U.S. sizes 5 and 7 (Continental sizes 4 and 5)
Or sizes needed to obtain gauge
Notions: Stitch holders, double-pointed needles *or* 16-inch circular needles, tapestry needle

GAUGE: With larger needles, in stockinette stitch, 5 stitches and 6 rows = 1 inch (2.5 centimeters)

FINISHED MEASUREMENTS:
Bust: 36 inches (91.5 centimeters) [38 inches (96.5 centimeters), 40 inches (101.5 centimeters)]
Sleeve (measured at underarm seam): 18 inches (45.5 centimeters) [19 inches (48 centimeters), 20 inches (50.75 centimeters)]
Length: 24 inches (61 centimeters) [25 inches (63.5 centimeters), 26 inches (66 centimeters)]

FRONT
With smaller needles, cast on 82 [84, 86] sts and work k1, p1 ribbing for 2 inches (5 centimeters). Change to larger needles and inc 10 [14, 18] sts, evenly spaced, across row (92 [98, 104] sts).

Work evenly in St st for 2 rows. Change to pattern. Work 1st 5 [8, 11] sts in St st, then 82 sts from chart, then last 5 [8, 11] sts in St st. Continue for the 123 rows of chart (approximately 18 inches [45.5 centimeters]). Continue to work in St st until front measures 22½ inches (57 centimeters), [23 inches (58.5 centimeters), 23½ inches (60.5 centimeters)] overall.

Shape neck: Work 38 [40, 43] sts, then put next 16 [18, 18] sts on holder. Join a new ball of yarn and work remaining 38 [40, 43] sts. At neck edge, at both sides, p2 tog 4 times on p row. Work evenly for 4 rows in St st.

Shape shoulders: At each armhole edge, bind off 9 [9, 10] sts twice; bind off 8 [9, 10] sts once; and bind off 8 [9, 9] sts once.

BACK

With smaller needles, cast on 82 [84, 86] sts and work in k1, p1 ribbing for 2 inches (5 centimeters). Change to larger needles and inc 10 [14, 18] sts, evenly spaced, across row (92 [98, 104] sts). Work in St st until back matches front before start of shoulder shaping.

Shape shoulders: Bind off loosely, at beginning of next 4 rows: 9 sts, 9 sts, 8 sts, 8 sts [9 sts, 9 sts, 9 sts, 9 sts; 10 sts, 10 sts, 10 sts, 9 sts] (24 [26, 26] sts remaining). Put remaining sts on holder.

SLEEVE

With smaller needles, cast on 40 [42, 44] sts and work in k1, p1 ribbing for 2½ inches (6.25 centimeters).

Change to larger needles and inc 26 sts, evenly spaced, across row (66 [68, 70] sts). Work evenly in St st. *At the same time,* inc 1 st, each side, every 1 inch (2.5 centimeters) 15 times. Continue to work evenly until sleeve measures 18 inches (45.5 centimeters) [19 inches (48 centimeters), 20 inches (50.75 centimeters)] overall (96 [98, 100] sts). Bind off loosely.

Work another sleeve in the same manner.

FINISHING

Join shoulder seams. Match top center of sleeve with the shoulder seam and join to front and back evenly. Join seam from bottom of sleeve to underarm, then from underarm down to bottom of sweater. With DPN, pick up 72 [76, 76] sts around neck. Beginning at top of right shoulder seam, pick up 16 sts to front holder; k 16 [18, 18] sts on front holder; pick up 16 sts to back holder; k 24 [26, 26] sts from back holder. Work in k1, p1 ribbing for 2 inches (5 centimeters).

Bind off loosely.

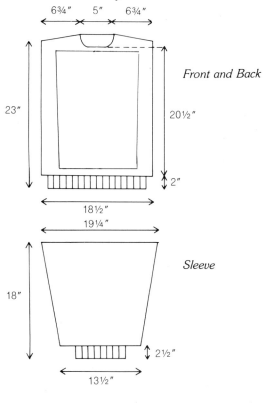

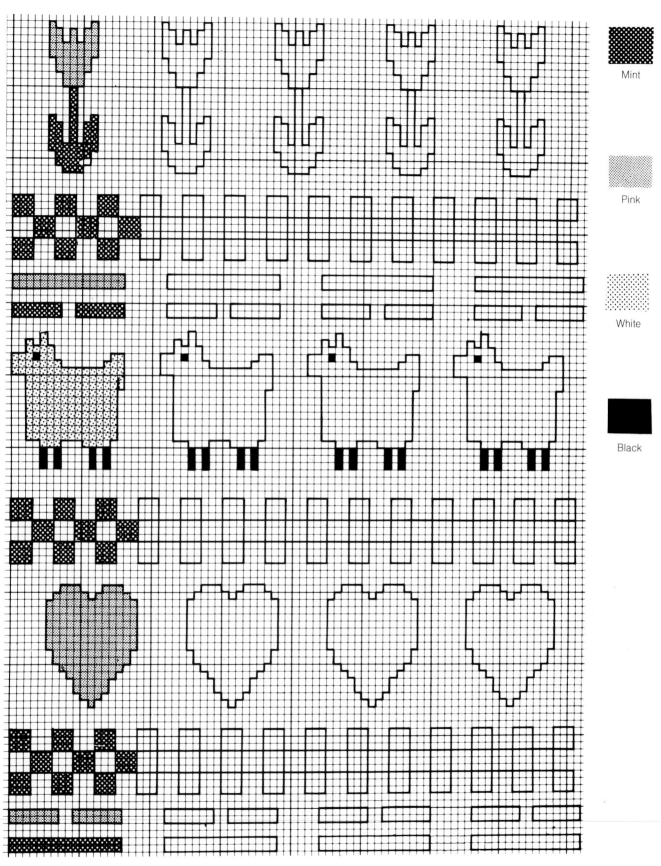

Mint

Pink

White

Black

115 rows = 17½"

129

HOW TO DO JAZZ-KNITTING

One of the simplest ways to try out the technique of changing colors is jazz-knitting—so called because it is a spontaneous, free-form method of changing as you go along. The sweater on page 132, shown in hand-dyed New Zealand wools, may be done by picking up and dropping colors as the spirit moves you. There should be some consistency to the pattern in order to hold everything together, and the predominant color should be thought of as the background. (The Nantucket Sweater on page 43 is worked in the same way, then embroidered after the sweater fabric is completed.)

This free-form style of knitting can be very effective whether it is done with a variety of textured yarns or with colors varied instead of textures. As you knit, join new colors at random. To keep a clean division between colors, be sure to join on the knit side, or face. On a purl row, a narrow stripe of the old color will appear above the first ridge of the new color. You will notice this effect on the back of your work if you join the new color on a knit row. Of course, the design may make an asset of the narrow stripe: If so, by all means let it appear on the face of the work.

When joining new yarns vertically, make sure to cross one with the other when they come together so that unsightly holes do not appear in the knitting (see diagram).

Try to join yarns at the beginning or end of a row. Attach each new yarn with a slip knot, leaving long ends. The ends can be woven into the seams when the garments are made up. If you must join a new yarn in the middle of a row, leave a length of the old yarn and an equal length of the new. After you have worked several rows, join the two ends with a square knot. Weave in the loose ends on the reverse side vertically so that they do not affect the stretch of the knitting.

Some knitters think the best way to join two yarns is by an alternative method, splicing. This is done by separating one ply from each yarn and twisting them together. The two twisted ends are then run into the back of the knitting vertically.

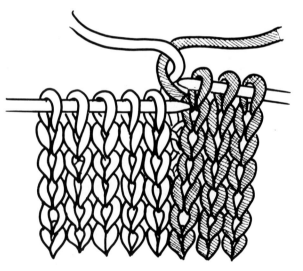

JAZZ SWEATER

The colors in this sweater—from whipped cream to dark chocolate—are all undyed, natural shades straight from the sheep's back! Lorna Boquest, who raises her own sheep and spins her own yarn in New Zealand, makes up the patterns for her sweaters as she goes along, in the true style of jazz-knitting. For a jazz sweater of your own, you can add raw silk or alpaca, or even combine textures and tones using wool-winding. You might begin by following the graph on page 134, and then try out your own shapes as you gain the confidence to experiment with jazz-knitting.

SIZES: Small [Medium, Large]

MATERIALS:
Yarn: Approximately 1,200 yards (1,100 meters) of bulky yarns or combinations, such as mohair and wool/silk or wool/alpaca/bulky twist

Needles: Straight knitting needles, U.S. sizes 7 and 9 (Continental sizes 5 and 6)
Circular needles, 24 inches (61 centimeters) and 40 inches (101.5 centimeters) long, U.S. size 7 (Continental size 5)
Or sizes needed to obtain gauge

Notions: Tapestry needle

GAUGE: With larger needles, in stockinette stitch, 3 stitches and 3 rows = 1 inch (2.5 centimeters). Gauge may vary with yarn of different thickness.

FINISHED MEASUREMENTS:
Bust: 42 inches (106.5 centimeters) [44 inches (111.75 centimeters), 48 inches (122 centimeters)]

Sleeve (measured at underarm seam): 21½ inches (57 centimeters)

Length: 24 inches (61 centimeters)

FRONT
With larger needles, cast on 76 [82, 84] sts and work in St st, following graph or your own random pattern, until front measures 16½ inches (42 centimeters)

Divide for neck: K38 [41, 42]; join new ball of yarn; k38 [41, 42]. Continue to work each side at the same time. Dec 1 st, every other row, at neck edge until front measures 22 inches (56 centimeters) overall (10 [12, 10] dec in all; 22 sts remain each side).

On next row, cast on 20 sts between shoulders to make 1 piece (64 sts). Continue with back.

BACK

Work back as straight piece, following graph until complete or your own random pattern for 82 rows. Bind off.

NECK

Sew shoulders together. Start at center front neck. With shorter circular needles, pick up 36 [38, 38] sts along left front neck, 24 [28, 32] sts along back neck, and 36 [38, 38] sts along right front neck (96 [104, 108] sts). Work k2, p2 ribbing for 8 rows. *At the same time,* k 2 tog, each side, every row. Bind off loosely in ribbing. Sew center seam of vee.

SLEEVE

With smaller needles, cast on 34 sts and work k2, p2 ribbing for 2 inches (5 centimeters). Change to larger needles. Working in St st, beg following graph or your own random pattern. On 1st row, inc 12 sts, evenly spaced (46 sts). Work evenly until sleeve measures 12 inches (30.5 centimeters) [13 inches (33 centimeters), 13½ inches (34.25 centimeters)] overall.

Inc 1 st, each side, next row and every 1 inch (2.5 centimeters) following 9 times (64 sts). Bind off loosely.

Work a second sleeve in the same manner.

RIBBING

Since you are using bulky yarn, knit the ribbing on circular needles to avoid a bulky seam. Pick up 144 sts around back and front of sweater and work k2,

p2 ribbing for 8 rounds, or until ribbing measures 2 inches (5 centimeters). Bind off loosely in ribbing.

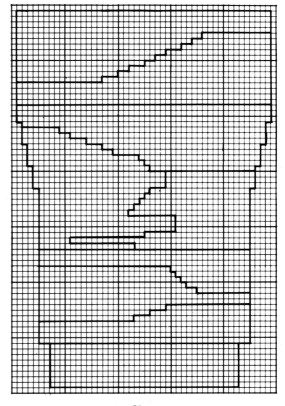

Sleeve

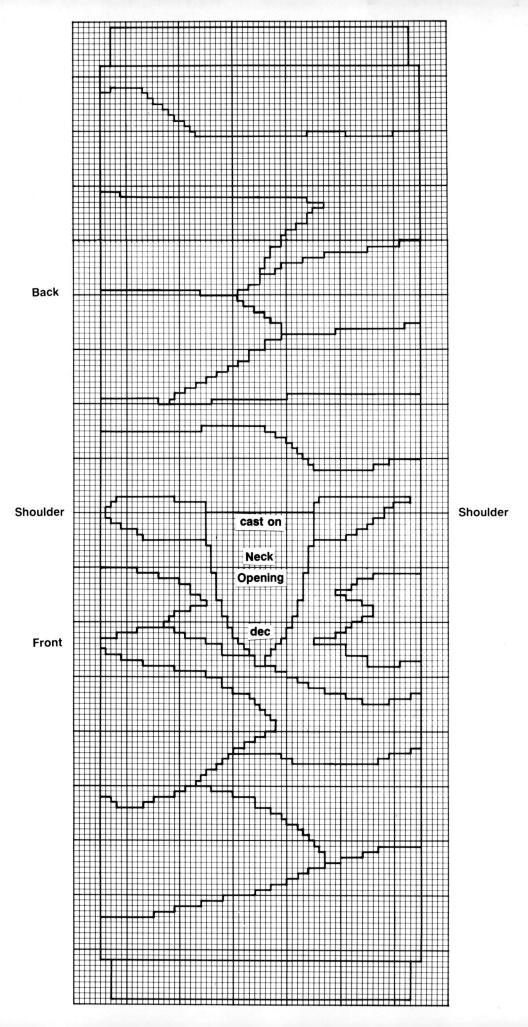

JAZZ KNITTING

Back

Shoulder

Front

cast on

Neck

Opening

dec

Shoulder

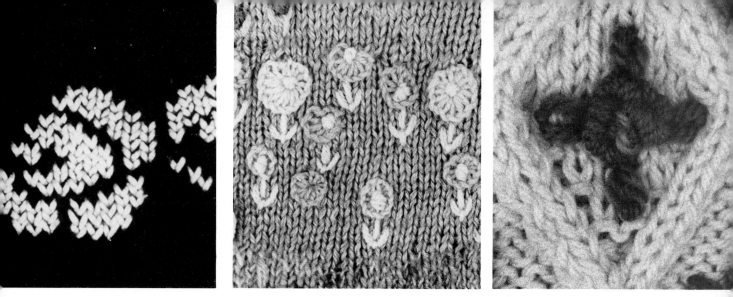

CREATIVE EMBELLISHMENTS

There are hundreds of exciting ways to express your own personality in your finished sweater. Metallic yarns or beads can add a shimmer to everything and transform even the simplest pullover into a glamorous evening ensemble. Or you can use needlework or embroidery as the added touch that turns your basic sweater into a masterpiece.

The Nantucket Sweater, with its wildflowers, sailboat, and seagulls, is an example of this. The design is drawn on tracing paper, and lazy-daisy stitches, French knots, and fishbone stitches are worked right through both the tracing paper and the knitting. When the stitching is complete, the fabric is torn away (see page 137). On the Tyrolean Embroidered Jacket, the texture of the knitting gives the position for the lazy-daisy flowers, so that they can be worked freehand.

Knitted appliqué is a very creative way to add interest to your knitting. Simply knit the decorative shapes and then stitch them or knit them in place, as shown for the Snakes and Ladders and Find the Letter cardigans (see page 40).

Duplicate stitch is embroidered with a tapestry needle. The knitting stitches are covered in a different color, so that the new color appears to be knitted in. The same patterns could be executed with intarsia (the method of changing colors as you knit), but duplicate stitch lets you decide on the shape and position of the design after the garment is knitted. For example, plaids can be made by first knitting horizontal bands of alternating colors and then adding vertical lines in duplicate stitch afterward. Use either duplicate stitch or intarsia to work the patterns on pages 152–153.

For a simple background for your creative embellishments, you may want to use the sweater on page 127. Knit it without the Sheep and Hearts pattern and increase or decrease it in size as you desire.

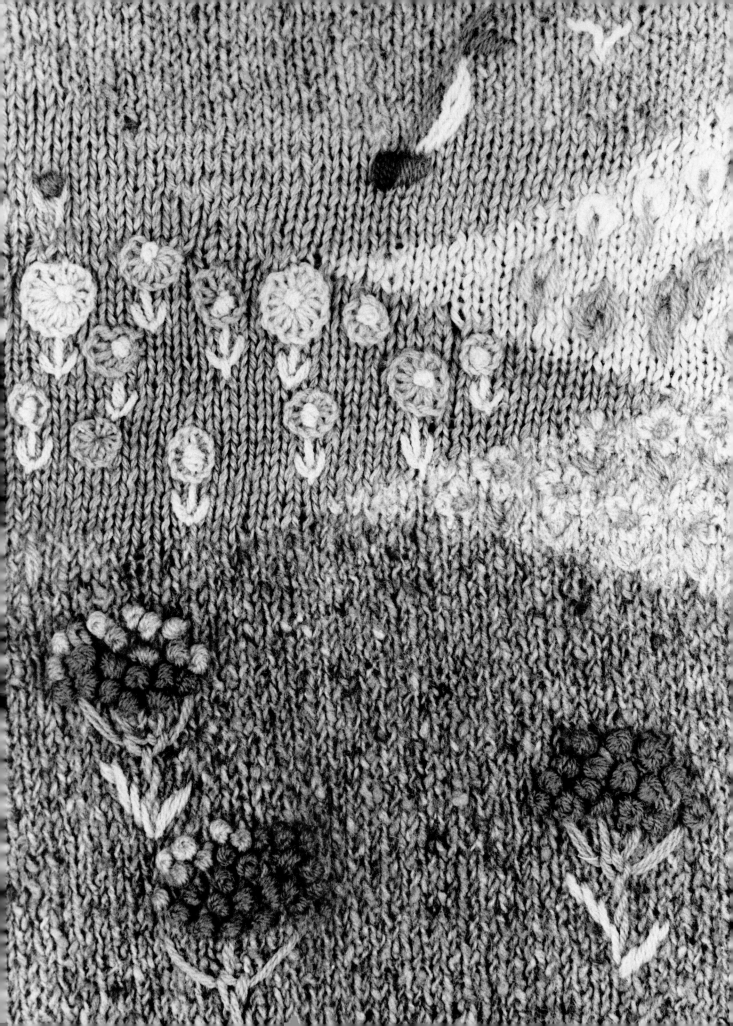

HOW TO EMBROIDER YOUR FINISHED SWEATER

Embroidery stitches may be added to create a repeat pattern, following the texture of your knitting (as for the Tyrolean Jacket on page 49), or done freely in an overall design that becomes a focal part of the sweater (as for the Nantucket Sweater on page 43).

To do the embroidery, first mount some muslin or tulle (fine net) on stretcher strips a little larger than the sweater shape you are embroidering. (Stretcher strips are available in all sizes from art supply stores.) Staple the fabric taut in the frame, stretching firmly. Then baste the sweater shape down on top. (It is much easier to embroider each piece separately before assembling your sweater.) Use the very long basting stitch, shown below, which is designed to keep everything flat. Center the sweater shape in the middle of the frame.

Next, enlarge and trace the design on tissue paper or tulle. Lay the tracing faceup on top of the sweater shape and lightly baste or pin-baste in place. Embroider the stitches, following the diagrams on page 140. Stab the needle straight up and down through the three layers—tracing layer, knitting, and muslin layer. When the stitching is complete, tear away the tracing layer all around the design. Ease out the small pieces left under the stitching with a blunt tapestry needle. Tearing away is easier if you pull sharply in vertical strips between the stitches. Tweezers are a help for removing small scraps. On the reverse side, trim away the muslin all around, close to the design, on both sides of the stitching. Assemble the sweater following the instructions for the Sheep and Hearts Sweater (page 127).

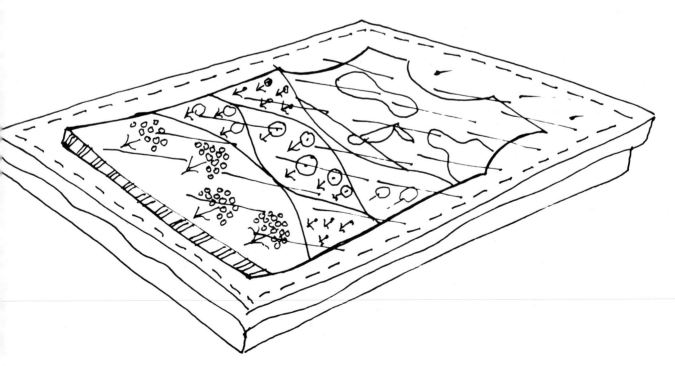

NANTUCKET SWEATER

(Color photo page 43)

You may embroider this sweater with flowers, sailboat, and seagulls, as it is shown here, or stitch it with shells, fish, and boats on a background of shades of blue, as though seen through layers of water; or even adapt it to a farm scene with trees and houses, sheep and cows—let your imagination fly!

SIZES: Small [Medium, Large]

MATERIALS:

Yarn: Knitting lightweight worsted, such as Anny Blatt's Dallas (the original was knitted in Tahki Donegal and Candide tweedy yarn)

For back, sleeves, and ribbing: 1,000 yards (915 meters) of medium blue

For sky: 1 ball of pale blue

For clouds: 1 ball of very pale blue angora

For sea: 1 ball of medium blue

For dunes and shore: mixture of deep pink, lavender, pale pink, and deep lavender

Needles: Straight knitting needles, U.S. sizes 5 and 7 (Continental sizes 4 and 5)

Or sizes needed to obtain gauge

Notions: 3 yards (2.75 meters) muslin fabric, stretcher strips (see page 137), sewing thread, number 16 chenille needle, tapestry needle

GAUGE: With larger needles, in stockinette stitch, 3 stitches and 4 rows = 1 inch (2.5 centimeters)

FINISHED MEASUREMENTS:

Bust: 42 inches (106.5 centimeters) [44 inches (111.75 centimeters), 48 inches (122 centimeters)]

Sleeve (measured at underarm seam): 19 inches (48 centimeters)

Length: 25 inches (63.5 centimeters)

Refer to page 140 for embroidery stitches.

Follow instructions for the Jazz Sweater, page 132, counting out front pattern from graph shown opposite; or use the basic crewneck sweater, the Sheep and Hearts, on page 127, following graph on this page for front and sleeves *only*.

Colors

H gray SuperKid 1012

J light blue 203

A blue 204

B and F pink 206

C light lavender 227

D and E tan 119

G pink lavender 228

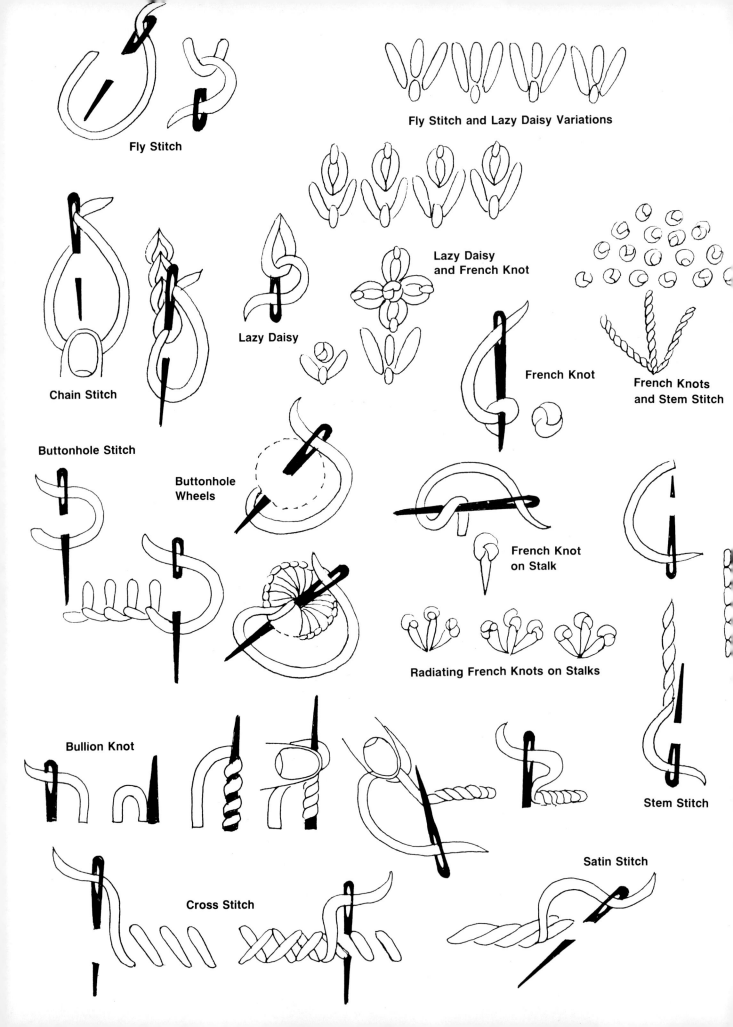

Fly Stitch

Fly Stitch and Lazy Daisy Variations

Lazy Daisy and French Knot

Chain Stitch

Lazy Daisy

French Knot

French Knots and Stem Stitch

Buttonhole Stitch

Buttonhole Wheels

French Knot on Stalk

Radiating French Knots on Stalks

Bullion Knot

Stem Stitch

Satin Stitch

Cross Stitch

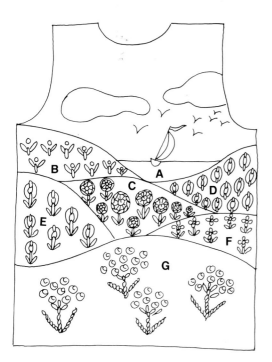

G: Using 6 strands, work fly-stitch upper stalks in medium green; work stem-stitch lower stalks in pale green; work French knots in three shades of pink.

When embroidery is complete, assemble sweater following instructions for the Jazz Sweater (page 132) or the Sheep and Hearts Sweater (page 127).

Key

A=cloud (left sleeve)
B=cloud (right sleeve)

Sleeve

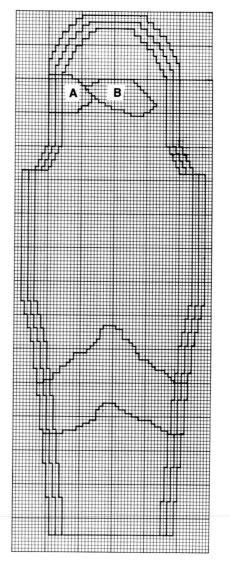

Before assembling sweater, work the embroidery as described on page 137 and shown above and opposite, using 3-ply Persian needlepoint yarn and number 16 chenille needle. Use 3 strands of yarn unless otherwise noted.

A: Work sailboat and pennant in satin stitch; mast and sail in stem stitch; seagulls in stem stitch.

B: Using 6 strands, work French knots in deep pink; fly stitch in pale pink.

C: Using 3 strands, work buttonhole wheels in pale apricot; French knot in pale green at center; work fly-stitch stalks in pale green.

D: Using 6 strands, work lazy daisy in pale pink; work single satin stitch stems in pink-beige.

E: Using 6 strands, work lazy daisy in pale pink; work fly-stitch stalks in pink-beige.

F: Work lazy daisy in pale apricot, forming 4 petals; work French knot in deep pink at center; work fly-stitch stalks in pale pink.

141

BANDS, BORDERS, AND BULLIONS

Borders and bands are perfect foils for embroidery stitches—the needlework adds a finishing touch to the textured knitting. Bullion knots and lazy daisy are ideal stitches to combine with bands for the Tyrolean Jacket on page 49 or the Skye Sampler Sweater on page 55.

TEXTURED KNITTING STITCHES
Moss Stitch This pattern is worked on a multiple of 2 sts.

ROW 1: *K1, p1; repeat from * across row.

ROW 2 (ON EVEN NUMBER OF STS): *P1, k1; repeat from * across row.

ROW 2 (ON ODD NUMBER OF STS): *K1, p1; repeat from * across row.

Alternate these 2 rows for pattern st.

Lozenge Pattern: This pattern is worked on a multiple of 18 sts (not including selvedge sts).

ROWS 1 AND 3: P7, k4, p7.

ROW 2 (AND ALL EVEN ROWS): Work sts as facing, knitting the k sts and purling the p sts.

ROW 5: P7; sl next 2 sts onto cable needle and hold in front of work; k2; k 2 sts from cable needle; p 7.

ROW 7: P6; sl next st onto cable needle and hold in back of work; k2; p 1 st from cable needle (twist 3 sts to right); sl next 2 sts to cable needle and hold in front of work; p1; k 2 sts from cable needle (twist 3 sts to left); p6.

ROW 9: P5; twist 3 sts to right; k2; twist 3 sts to left; p5.

ROW 11: P4; twist 3 sts to right; k4; twist 3 sts to left; p4.

ROW 13: P3; twist 3 sts to right; k6; twist 3 sts to left; p3.

ROW 15: P2; twist 3 sts to right; k8; twist 3 sts to left; p2.

ROW 17: P2; twist 3 sts to left; p1; k6; p1; twist 3 sts to right; p2.

ROW 19: P3; twist 3 sts to left; p1; k4; p1; twist 3 sts to right; p3.

ROW 21: P4; twist 3 sts to left; p1; k2; p1; twist 3 sts to right; p4.

ROW 23: P5; twist 3 sts to left; p2; twist 3 sts to right; p5.

ROW 25: P6; twist 3 sts to left; twist 3 sts to right; p6.

Repeat from Row 5 to form pattern.

Reverse Cable with Raised Ribbing
Border: This pattern is worked on a multiple of 12 sts plus 2 selvedge sts.

ROWS 1 AND 3: K1, p2, k8, p2, k1.

ROWS 2 AND 4: P1, k2, p8, k2, p1.

ROW 5: K1, p2, sl 2 sts onto cable needle and hold in back of work; k next 2 sts; k 2 sts from cable needle; sl next 2 sts to cable needle and hold in front of work; k next 2 sts; k 2 sts from cable needle; p2, k1.

Repeat from Row 2 to form pattern.

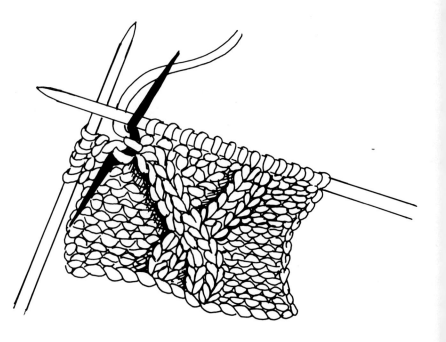

TYROLEAN EMBROIDERED JACKET
(Color photo page 49)

This classic design seems fresh and new, with its contemporary silhouette and bright embroidery. Knit it in light cream or natural, as shown, with dark, jewellike embroidery colors, or in black with brilliant contrasts for the stitchery.

SIZES: Small [Medium]

MATERIALS:
Yarn: 2,000 yards (1,830 meters) of ecru worsted weight

Needles: Straight knitting needles, U.S. sizes 3 and 5 (Continental sizes 3 and 4)

Crochet hook, U.S. size D (Continental size 3)

Or sizes needed to obtain gauge

Notions: Tapestry needle

GAUGE: With larger needles, in moss stitch, 18 stitches and 33 rows = 4 inches (10 centimeters)

FINISHED MEASUREMENTS:
Bust: 39½ inches (100.25 centimeters) [42 inches (106.25 centimeters)]

Sleeve (measured at underarm seam): 17 inches (43 centimeters) [17½ inches (44.5 centimeters)]

Length: 20¼ inches (51.5 centimeters) [21¼ inches (54 centimeters)]

BACK
With smaller needles, cast on 110 [114] sts and work in k1, p1 ribbing for 2¾ inches (7 centimeters). Change to larger needles and work in moss st. Dec 20 [18] sts, evenly spaced, across first row (90 [96] sts). Work evenly in moss st until back measures 11¾ inches (30 centimeters) [12¼ inches (31 centimeters)] overall.

   Shape armholes: Bind off, each side, 9 [10] sts once (72 [76] sts). Work evenly until back measures 20¼ inches (51.5 centimeters) [21¼ inches (54 centimeters)] overall. Bind off sts.

RIGHT FRONT
With smaller needles, cast on 60 [63] sts and work k1, p1 ribbing for 2¾ inches (7 centimeters). Change to larger needles and work pattern as follows, beginning on RS side: Work across 7 [8] sts in moss st; k1, p2, k8 (= 1 cable);

p2; k1; p7, k4, p7 (= 1 lozenge); k1, p2, k8 (= 1 cable), p2; k1; work across 7 [9] sts in moss st. Continue in pattern, working pattern sts as established, until front measures 11¾ inches (30 centimeters) [12¼ inches (31 centimeters)] overall.

Shape armholes: Bind off, at left side, 9 [10] sts once (51 [53] sts). Continue evenly in pattern until front measures 18½ inches (47 centimeters) [19¼ inches (49 centimeters)] overall.

Shape neck: Bind off, at right side, every other row, 8 [9] sts once and 2 sts 6 times (31 [32] sts). Continue working evenly in pattern until front measures 20¼ inches (51.5 centimeters) [21¼ inches (54 centimeters)] overall. Bind off remaining sts.

LEFT FRONT

Work same as for right front, reversing shaping and beginning 1st row of pattern as follows: 7 [9] sts in moss st, then continue as established, ending 7 [8] sts moss st.

SLEEVE

With smaller needles, cast on 51 [55] sts and work k1, p1 ribbing for 2¼ inches (5.75 centimeters). Change to larger needles and work in moss st. Inc 9 sts, evenly spaced, across 1st row (60 [64] sts).

Shape sides: Inc 1 st, each side, every 12th row, 9 times (78 [82] sts). Work evenly in pattern until sleeve measures 17 inches (43 centimeters) [17½ inches (44.5 centimeters)] overall.

Shape cap: Bind off, each side, every other row, 2 sts 3 times and 1 st 19 times (28 [32] sts).

Bind off remaining sts.

Work another sleeve in the same manner.

FRONT BORDER

With smaller needles, cast on 7 sts and work k1, p1 ribbing for ⅜ inch (1 centimeter) [½ inch (1.25 centimeters)].

Make 1 buttonhole over 1 st (work 2 sts tog, yo) in center of border. Continue in ribbing. Make 6 more buttonholes, spaced 3 inches (7.5 centimeters) apart, in the same way. When border measures 18½ inches (47 centimeters) [19¼ inches (49 centimeters)] overall, bind off in ribbing. Work a second border, omitting buttonholes.

FINISHING

Embroider flowers as shown on page 140, referring to page 142 and color photograph on page 49. Round flowers are worked in bullion st. Other flowers and leaves are worked in detached chain stitch. Hearts of the flowers are worked in French knots. Join shoulder seams. Set sleeves in, gathering extra fullness at top. Join side and sleeve seams. Sew front borders on, matching corresponding sides.

Neckband: RS facing, with smaller needles, starting in middle of right front border, pick up 87 sts, evenly spaced, along neck edge. Work k1, p1 ribbing for ¾ inch (2 centimeters), and k 1 row on WS of work (folding line). Then work for another ¾ inch (2 centimeters) in ribbing. Bind off in ribbing. Fold neckband to outside and sl st in place.

With crochet hook, make 7 buttons, as follows: Ch 4 and join 4th ch to the 1st with a sl st. Work 8 dc into circle. Sl 1 ordinary button into crocheted button, then close button, as follows: Make 1 sc into each dc. Then work 1 round of 1 sc in 2 sc. Sew buttons opposite buttonholes.

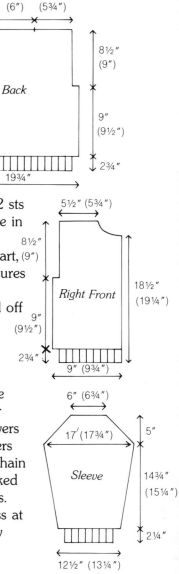

145

HOW TO DO DUPLICATE STITCH

This way of adding decorative patterns and motifs to your finished sweater is your special secret. Only *you* know that the design has been done on top afterward instead of knitted in. The stitch, as its name implies, duplicates the knitted stitch underneath, making it easy to knit a plain sweater and then plan the exact position of a design after the sweater is complete. On the facing page and following pages are some ideas for you to try—the Evening Rose and Autumn Leaves sweaters.

If you are working with angora, instead of placing the stitches side by side, you can space them out, covering every other stitch and working diagonally. This gives a fluffier, lighter effect, which is most attractive with this yarn.

Designs may be worked out on graphs and then counted out onto the sweater. Pattern books for needlepoint and cross stitch with graphed designs are easily available and may be used for duplicate-stitch designs, too. Draw them with colored pencils on the knitter's graph paper (page 176) to establish the proportions of the design when knitted (and save a lot of unpicking later).

To give a distinctly "added" (not knitted in) effect, use cross stitch instead of duplicate stitch, counting the design out on the background of the sweater as though it were embroidery linen.

You may also combine duplicate stitch with embroidery stitches (as is done with the Autumn Leaves Sweater on page 150) for a clear-cut, outlined effect.

Bring needle up at the base of the stitch to be covered.

Pass the needle from right to left under 2 loops of the same stitch 1 row above.

Reinsert needle into base of the original stitch.

Pull each stitch gently to maintain the tension of the original knitting, completely covering the knitted stitch with the new color.

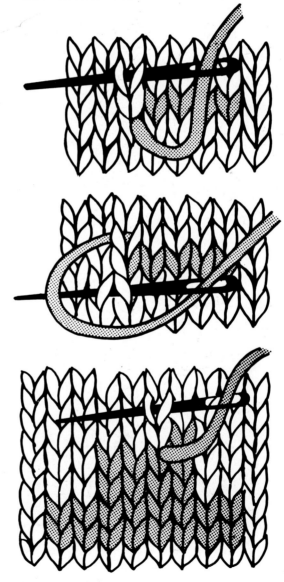

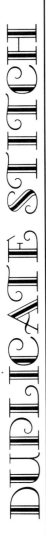

DUPLICATE STITCH

EVENING ROSE SWEATER

Champagne silk ribbon is used for the duplicate stitch on a black mohair sweater. Imagine the roses in crimson on dove gray, or chalk white on delft blue. Duplicate stitch gives you the freedom to choose your embroidery color *after* the sweater is finished.

SIZES: Small [Medium, Large]

MATERIALS:

Yarn: Ten [eleven, twelve] 1½-ounce (40-gram), 110-yard (100-meter) balls of Reynolds's Saint Tropez black *(main color) or* mohair/silk blend

plus

1 ball of Reynolds's Pizzazz beige *(contrasting color) or* rayon

Needles: Straight knitting needles, U.S. sizes 5 and 7 (Continental sizes 3¾ and 4½)

Or sizes needed to obtain gauge

Notions: Tapestry needle, shoulder pads (if desired), scraps of interfacing (to back roses)

GAUGE: With larger needles and stockinette stitch, 18 stitches and 22 rows = 4 inches (10 centimeters)

FINISHED MEASUREMENTS:

Bust: 42 inches (106.5 centimeters) [46 inches (117 centimeters), 52 inches (132 centimeters)]

Sleeve (measured at underarm seam): 14½ inches (36.75 centimeters) [15 inches (38 centimeters), 15½ inches (39.5 centimeters)]

Length: 20 inches (50.75 centimeters) [20½ inches (52 centimeters), 21 inches (53.5 centimeters)]

BACK

With smaller needles and main color, cast on 72 [82, 90] sts and work k1, p1 ribbing for 2 inches (5 centimeters). Change to larger needles. Working in St st, inc 1 st, each side, every row 0 [0, 6] times, then every other row 11 [11, 8] times (94 [104, 118] sts). Back should measure approximately 6 inches (15.25 centimeters) overall.

Mark beginning and end of last row for armholes. Work evenly in St st until armhole measures 14 inches

(35.5 centimeters) [14½ inches (36.75 centimeters), 15 inches (38 centimeters)]. End with WS row.

Shape shoulder and neck: K27 [32, 36] sts; join a second ball of yarn and bind off center 40 [40, 46] sts; k to end. Working both sides separately at the same time, bind off from each shoulder 9 [10, 12] sts twice, then 9 [12, 12] sts once.

FRONT

Work same as for back until front measures 19 inches (48 centimeters) [19½ inches (49.5 centimeters), 20 inches (50.75 centimeters)] overall. End with a WS row.

Shape shoulders and neck: K34 [39, 44] sts; join a second ball of yarn and bind off center 26 [26, 30] sts; k to end. Working both sides separately at the same time, bind off from each neck edge 3 [3, 4] sts twice, then 1 st 1 [1, 0] time. *At the same time,* when same length as back to shoulder, shape shoulder as for back.

SLEEVE

With smaller needles and main color, cast on 46 sts and work k1, p1 ribbing for 2 inches (5 centimeters).
Change to larger needles. Working in St st, inc 1 st, each side, every row, 14 [16, 16] times, then every other row 26 [26,

28] times (126 [130, 134] sts). Work even if necessary until sleeve measures 14½ inches (36.75 centimeters) [15 inches (38 centimeters), 15½ inches (39.5 centimeters)], or desired sleeve length.
Bind off.
Work another sleeve in the same manner.

FINISHING

Block pieces to correct measurements. Cut interfacing approximately 5 inches (12.5 centimeters) square and place on WS of front randomly, as backing for duplicate stitch. After working duplicate stitch (see page 147), cut excess interfacing from back of work. Sew left shoulder seam.

Neckband: With RS facing, smaller needles, and main color, beg at right shoulder. Pick up and k 40 [40, 46] sts evenly around back neck edge, and 46 [46, 52] sts around front neck edge (86 [86, 98] sts).
Next row (WS): Purl. Continue to work in St st for 1 inch (2.5 centimeters). Bind off with larger needles, knitwise. Neckband will roll naturally.
Sew right shoulder seam, including neckband.
Sew top of sleeves to front and back between markers.
Sew side and sleeve seams.

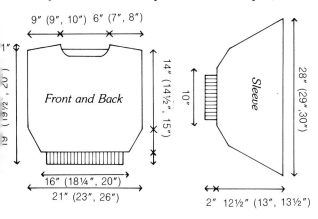

AUTUMN LEAVES SWEATER

(Color photo page 47)

This sweater gives the effect of appliquéd knitting because the leaf shapes (which may be either knitted in or done with duplicate stitch) are outlined with bold chain stitch to give them definition. Combining embroidery stitches with intarsia knitting adds another dimension to your design.

SIZE: One size fits Small/Medium

MATERIALS:

Yarn: Thirteen 1¾-ounce (50-gram) balls of Anny Blatt's Bright'Anny Tulipe (burgundy) *(main color)*
plus leaves assorted colors
One ball each of the following colors of mohair and silk:
Prune (dark purple-red) *(A)*
Olive (olive-green) *(B)*
Daim (buff) *(C)*
Fuchsia (hot pink) *(D)*

Needles: Straight knitting needles, U.S. sizes 5, 6, and 10 (Continental sizes 4, 4½, and 6½)

Or sizes needed to obtain gauge

Notions: Tapestry needle, 2 buttons

GAUGE: With largest needles, in stockinette stitch, 14 stitches and 18 rows = 4 inches (10 centimeters)

FINISHED MEASUREMENTS:

Bust: 42½ inches (108 centimeters)
Sleeve (measured at underarm seam): 16¾ inches (42.5 centimeters)
Length: 26½ inches (67.25 centimeters)

BACK

With medium-sized needles and main color, cast on 73 sts and work k1, p1 ribbing for 2½ inches (6.25 centimeters). Change to larger needles. Working in St st, inc 1 st in center of 1st row (74 sts). Work evenly until back measures 16¼ inches (41.25 centimeters) overall.

Shape armholes: Bind off, each side, every other row, 2 sts once and 1 st once (68 sts). Continue to work evenly until back measures 26½ inches (67.25 centimeters) overall.

Shape shoulders: Bind off, each side, every other row, 8 sts twice and 7 sts

150

once. *At the same time:* with 2nd shoulder dec, leave center 20 sts on holder for back neck.
Finish each side separately, binding off 1 st at neck edge after 2 rows.
Work other side in the same way, reversing shaping.

FRONT

Knit leaves in as you go, following chart, page 152, and using bobbin method (see page 125) *or* work leaves afterward in duplicate stitch. Work same as for back until front measures 18¾ inches (47.5 centimeters) overall.

Shape front placket opening: Bind off center 4 sts and continue each side separately over remaining 32 sts at each side. Continue to work evenly in St st until front measures 22¾ inches (58.75 centimeters) overall.
Shape neck: Bind off, at neck edge, every other row, 1 st once, 2 sts twice, 1 st three times, and then 1 st after 4 rows.
When front measures 26½ inches (67.25 centimeters) overall,
Shape shoulders as for back.
Work other side in same way, reversing shaping.

SLEEVE

With medium-sized needles and main color, cast on 45 sts and work k1, p1 ribbing for 2½ inches (6.25 centimeters). Change to larger needles. Working in St st, inc 1 st at center of 1st row (46 sts).
Shape sleeve: Inc 1 st, each side, every 4th row, 13 times (72 sts).
When sleeve measures 16¾ inches (42.5 centimeters) overall,
Shape cap: Bind off, each side, every other row, 2 sts once and 1 st once (66 sts).
Bind off remaining sts.
Work another sleeve in same manner.

BUTTON BANDS

With smallest needles and color A, cast on 9 sts and work k1, p1 ribbing for 4 inches (10 centimeters). Bind off. Make second button band in same way, but, at 1¼ inches (3 centimeters) and 3¼ inches (8.25 centimeters) from the beginning, work 2 buttonholes in middle of band as follows: k 2 tog, yo.

FINISHING

If sweater has been knitted plain, embroider leaves in duplicate stitch, following chart. Then embroider stems and outline leaves using chain stitch (see page 140).
Join shoulder seams.
Sew button and buttonhole bands along each edge of placket opening. Sew at middle of front, placing buttonhole band over button band and sewing through all 3 thicknesses.

Collar: RS facing, with smallest needles, beginning in middle of button band, pick up 87 sts around neck edge. With color A, work k1, p1 ribbing for 2¾ inches (7 centimeters). Bind off.
Set sleeves in.
Join side and sleeve seams.
Sew buttons opposite buttonholes.

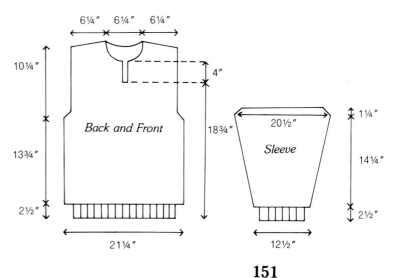

151

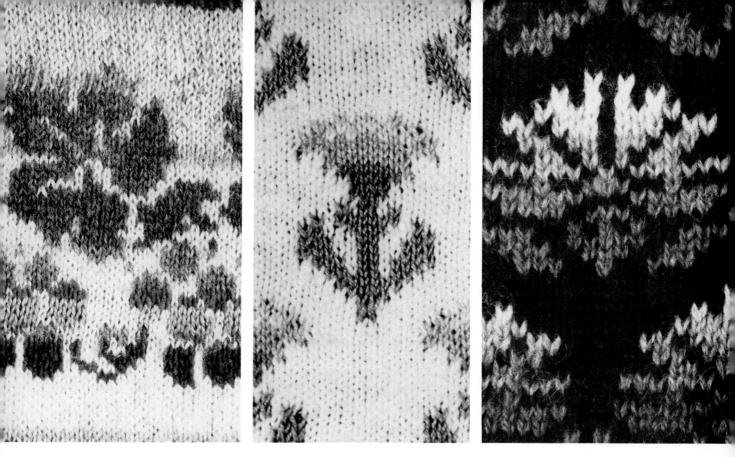

Patterns for Knitting in Intarsia or Duplicate Stitch

Graph for Autumn Leaves Sweater opposite.

CHILD'S "FIND THE LETTER" SWEATER
(Color photo page 40)

First knit the sweater with contrasting-color squares; then knit flaps to button over them. Finally, in duplicate stitch, embroider letters and numbers under the flaps. If you prefer, use double-knitting to make real pockets and tuck a tiny spool-knit animal (see page 159) in each one.

SIZES: Child's 1 [3, 6, 8, 10]

MATERIALS:

Yarn: Emu Superwash wool (50-gram balls)

    4 balls of green *(A)*
    1 ball of white *(B)*
    1 ball of yellow *(C)*
    a small amount of red *(D)*

Needles: Straight knitting needles, U.S. sizes 3 and 5 (Continental sizes 3¼ and 4)
Or sizes needed to obtain gauge

Notions: Stitch holders, tapestry needle, 17 [17, 19, 19, 21] small buttons

GAUGE: With larger needles, in stockinette stitch, 11 stitches and 15 rows = 2 inches (5 centimeters)

FINISHED MEASUREMENTS:

Chest: 22 inches (56 centimeters) [24 inches (61 centimeters), 26½ inches (66.25 centimeters), 28 inches (71 centimeters), 30 inches (77.5 centimeters)]

Sleeve (measured at underarm seam): 7½ inches (19 centimeters) [8 inches (20 centimeters), 9 inches (23 centimeters), 11½ inches (29.25 centimeters), 13 inches (33 centimeters)]

Length: 13 inches (33 centimeters) [13½ inches (34.25 centimeters), 15 inches (38 centimeters), 16½ inches (42 centimeters), 17 inches (43 centimeters)]

BACK

With smaller needles and color A, cast on 61 [65, 73, 77, 83] sts and work k1, p1 ribbing for 1½ inches (3.75 centimeters).

On the last row of ribbing, *for sizes 3 and 8 only,* inc 1 st at middle of row (61 [66, 73, 78, 83] sts).

Change to larger needles. Work evenly in St st until back measures 13 inches (33 centimeters) [13½ inches (34.25 centimeters), 15 inches (38 centimeters), 16½ inches (42 centimeters), 17 inches (43 centimeters)] overall. End with p row.

Change to smaller needles. K 5 rows.

Next row: Bind off 19 [21, 23, 25, 27] sts; k next 22 [23, 26, 27, 28] sts; bind off remaining 19 [21, 23, 25, 27] sts. Cut off yarn.

With RS facing, rejoin color A to sts on needle. K 3 rows.

FRONT

With smaller needles and color A, cast on 61 [65, 73, 77, 83] sts and work k1, p1 ribbing for 1½ inches (3.75 centimeters).

On the last row of ribbing, *for sizes 3 and 8 only,* inc 1 st at center of last row (61 [66, 73, 78, 83] sts).

Change to larger needles. Work evenly in St st for 10 [12, 14, 16, 18] rows.

Wind color B into 3 separate balls. Join on and cut off yarns as required, twisting yarns on wrong side of work when changing color to avoid making holes.

ROW 1 (RS): K 9 [11, 13, 15, 15] color A; *8 color B, 10 [10, 12, 12, 14] color A; repeat from *; 8 color B; k to end with color A.

ROW 2: P 8 [11, 12, 15, 16] color A; *8 color B, 10 [10, 12, 12, 14] color A; repeat from *; 8 color B; p to end with color A.

ROWS 3-8: Work 1st and 2nd rows 3 times.

ROW 9: Repeat 1st row.

ROW 10: P with color A.

ROW 11: With color A, k9 [11, 13, 15, 15]; *p8, k10 [10, 12, 12, 14]; repeat from *; p8; k to end.

ROWS 12-20 [12-22, 12-24, 12-28, 12-28]: Beginning with p row, work in St st.

Repeat last 20 [22, 24, 28, 28] rows once. Then work Rows 1–11 again. Cut off color B.

Continue to work evenly in St st, using color A only, until front measures 11 inches (28 centimeters) [11½ inches (29.25 centimeters), 13 inches (33 centimeters), 14½ inches (36.75 centimeters), 15 inches (38 centimeters)] overall. End with p row.

Divide for neck: K22 [24, 27, 29, 31]. Put remaining sts on holder. Turn work. Dec 1 st, at neck edge, *every other row*, until 19 [21, 23, 25, 27] sts remain. Work evenly in St st until front measures 13 inches (33 centimeters) [13½ inches (34.25 centimeters), 15 inches (38 centimeters), 16½ inches (42 centimeters), 17 inches (43 centimeters)] overall, ending at neck edge. Change to smaller needles. K 3 rows.

Buttonhole row: K4 [4, 3, 2, 2]; *k 2 tog, yo, k 3 [4, 3, 4, 3] sts; repeat from * once [once, twice, twice, 3 times]; k 2 tog, yo, k3. K 4 rows. Bind off. Return to sts on holder. Leave 1st 17 [18, 19, 20, 21] sts on holder. Put rest of sts on larger-sized needle, with needle tip at neck edge. Join color A and k to end of row.

Work to match other side of neck up to beginning of shoulder edge, ending at side edge.

Change to smaller needles. K 3 rows.

Buttonhole row: K3; *yo, k 2 tog, k3 [4, 3, 4, 3]; repeat from * once [once, twice, twice, 3 times]; yo, k 2 tog, k4 [4, 3, 2, 2]. K 4 rows. Bind off.

Neckband (RS): Join color A to neck at left front shoulder edging. With smaller needles, pick up and k 11 [11, 12, 14, 16] sts down left side of front neck; k front neck sts from holder; pick up and k 11 [11, 12, 14, 16] sts

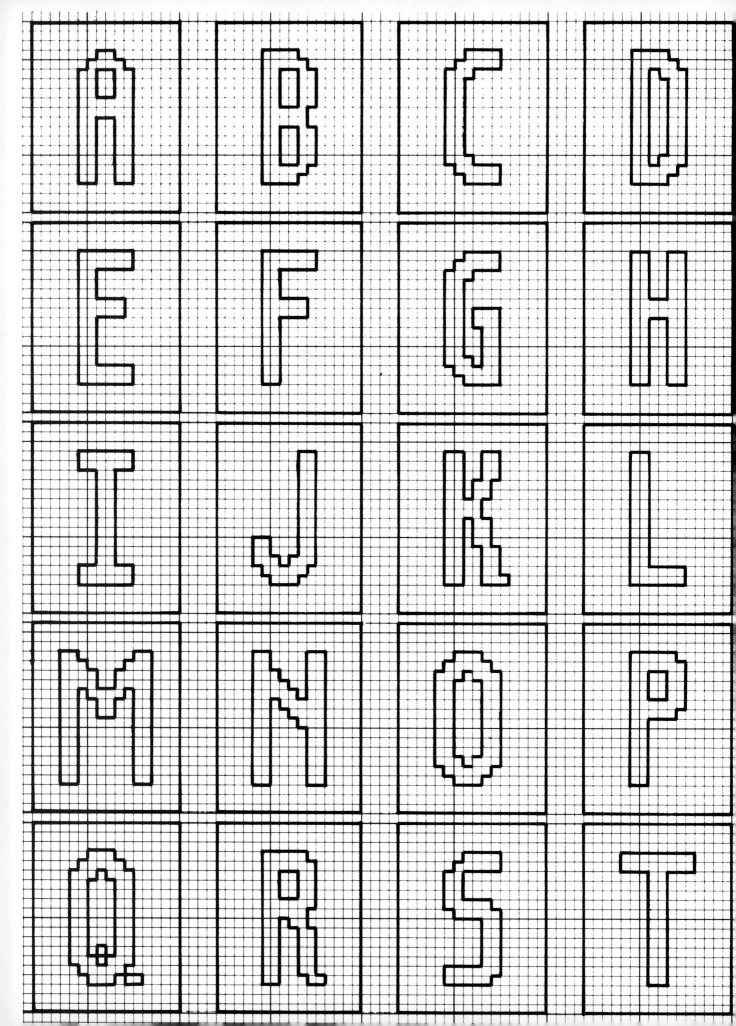

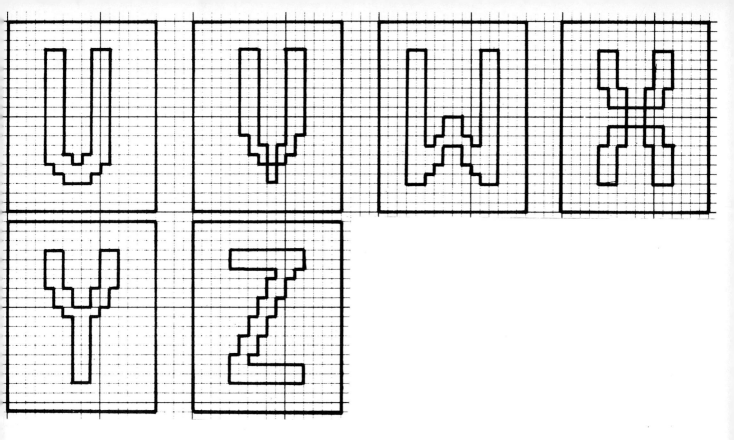

up right side of front neck to top of shoulder edging (39 [40, 43, 48, 53] sts). K 1 row.

Buttonhole row: K3, yo, k 2 tog, k to last 5 sts, k 2 tog, yo, k3. K 4 rows. Bind off.

SLEEVE

With smaller needles and color A, cast on 34 [36, 38, 38, 40] sts and work k1, p1 ribbing for 1½ inches (3.75 centimeters).

Change to larger needles. Working in St st, inc 1 st, each side, next and every following 3rd [3rd, 3rd, 4th, 4th] row, until there are 56 [60, 66, 72, 76] sts. Continue to work evenly in St st until sleeve measures 7½ inches (19 centimeters) [8 inches (20 centimeters), 9 inches (23 centimeters), 11½ inches (29.25 centimeters), 13 inches (33 centimeters)] overall.
Bind off. Work another sleeve in the same manner.

FLAP

With RS of front facing and cast-on edge uppermost, join color C to one square. With larger needles, pick up and k 1 st from each of the 8 ridge loops on the square's edge. P 1 row. Then k 11 rows. Bind off. Work flap for each square in the same manner. With color D, in duplicate st, embroider a letter or number on each square (under flap). Work a button loop in center of upper edge of flap. Attach button to corresponding spot on square. (Flaps open up.)

FINISHING

Lap front shoulder edgings over back and sew together at shoulders. Mark depth of armholes 5 inches (12.5 centimeters) [5½ inches (14 centimeters), 6 inches (15.25 centimeters), 6½ inches (16.5 centimeters), 7 inches (17.75 centimeters)] from shoulders on back and front. Set in sleeves between markers, then join side and sleeve seams. Sew on buttons.

TEXTURED EFFECTS— SMOCKING, SPOOL-KNITTING, AND APPLIQUÉ

Smocking, spool knitting, and appliqué are three methods for adding lively textured effects to your knitting.

SMOCKING

Smocking on fabric is a way of controlling gathers with decorative stitching. Gathers, in the form of vertical pleats, are stitched in pairs so that when stretched open, they form diamonds, like a honeycomb. In knitting, the pleats are made with ribbing, which is sewn together with the smocking, using either a contrasting or a matching color. Either way, a most interesting textural effect is obtained. Always allow half as much width again as the finished measurement to accommodate the fullness gathered up with the smocking.

RIBBING This pattern is worked on multiples of 3 sts.
ROW 1 AND ALTERNATE ROWS: *K1, p2; repeat from * across row.
ROW 2 AND ALTERNATE ROWS: *K2, p1; repeat from * across row.

When sufficient ribbing is knitted, work this spot-honeycomb-embroidery stitch in a matching or contrasting color. Use a blunt tapestry needle to avoid splitting threads.

Start at the left. Take one stitch over the first two ribs together. Then take a second stitch, but slide the needle right through the rib (see diagram at right).

Come out slightly to the left and above on the right side of the pair of ribs. Then take a stitch over this and the next rib together, but slide the needle *down* to come out slightly to the left of the rib, level with the first stitch taken.

Continue wrapping pairs of ribs together along the row. Care must be taken to make the two stitches come up and go down in the same hole, so that they appear to be one.

On the next row, take one rib from the first pair and one from the second pair. Wrap these together. This gives the honeycomb effect.

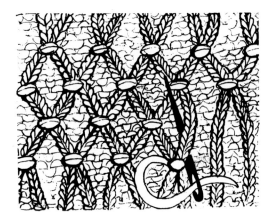

APPLIQUÉ

The art of appliqué—stitching one piece of fabric on top of another—is ideal for knitting, because seam allowances are never necessary and the shapes may be sewn on just as they are, with tiny hemming stitches and matching cotton floss. Shapes such as Humpty-Dumpty (see page 41) may be sewn down and embroidered details added later. Some shapes, like Humpty's bow tie, may be left loose to give a three-dimensional effect. Rings of petals, for example, could be stitched one on top of the other to form a raised flower. Crocheted shapes may be appliquéd instead of knitted ones.

SPOOL-KNITTING
Spool-knitting is done on a small cylindrical tool called a *knitting noddy* or *nancy.* Nails or pegs placed at regular intervals around the central hole at the top of this tool enable you to loop the yarn over to make a tube of knitting. The resulting length can then be sewn down as a decorative finish on a knitted fabric, such as the Snakes and Ladders Cardigan shown on page 40.

If it is impossible to find the correct tool, use an old bobbin or thread holder and hammer in the four nails yourself around the top. Use nails with smooth tops instead of broad, round heads.

Using a blunt needle, begin by threading yarn from the bottom to the top, through the hole in the cylinder.

Wind the yarn from left to right, once around the outside of the nails or pegs.

As you wind the yarn around the nails or pegs again, one at a time, lift the

lower loop of yarn over the upper strand and over the nail or peg.

Continue around and around, lifting one strand over another until a narrow tube appears at the bottom of the cylinder. Pull it down as you go.

To change color, knot a new strand of yarn and continue, making sure that the ends are buried inside the tube.

To end off, pass each loop over the next stitch to the right until only one stitch remains. Draw the yarn through the last stitch, pull it tightly, and run the end through the center of the tube.

159

SMOCKED DRESS

Simple and understated, this country dress with its smocked yoke is delightfully old-fashioned, straight out of a nursery rhyme. The smocking may be done in a contrasting color, as shown on p. 158, or—for a subtle effect—in a shade to match the dress.

SIZES: Child's 1 [3, 6, 8]

MATERIALS:

Yarn: Emu Superwash (50-gram balls) 5 to 7 balls of white *(main color) plus small amount of contrasting color, for smocking stitches*

Needles: Straight knitting needles, U.S. sizes 3, 4, and 5 (Continental sizes 3¼, 3¾, and 4) *Or sizes needed to obtain gauge*

Notions: Tapestry needle, 4 buttons, safety pin

GAUGE: With larger needles, in stockinette stitch, 11 stitches = 2 inches (5 centimeters)

FINISHED MEASUREMENTS:

Chest: 20 inches (50.75 centimeters) [22 inches (56 centimeters), 24 inches (61 centimeters), 26 inches (66 centimeters)]

Sleeve (measured at underarm seam): 8 inches (20 centimeters) [9½ inches (24 centimeters), 10½ inches (26.5 centimeters), 11½ inches (29.25 centimeters)]

Length: 25 inches (63.5 centimeters) [27½ inches (70 centimeters), 32 inches (81 centimeters), 33 inches (83.75 centimeters)]

BACK

With medium-sized needles, cast on 92 [96, 102, 108] sts and work 4 rows St st. Change to largest needles.

Picot row: K1, *yo, k 2 tog; repeat from * to end of row. Beginning with a p row, work evenly in St st until back measures 15 inches (38 centimeters) [16½ inches (42 centimeters), 19 inches (48 centimeters), 19 inches (48 centimeters)] overall. Work evenly for another 5 inches (12.5 centimeters) [5½ inches (14 centimeters), 7 inches (17.75 centimeters), 7½ inches (19 centimeters)]. End with p row; mark end of row with colored thread or another marker.

Dec row: K1 [3, 6, 9] sts, [k 2 tog, k1] 30 times, k1 [3, 6, 9] (62 [66, 72, 78] sts). Beginning with p row, k 5 rows St st, ending with p row.

Shape armholes: Bind off 2 [3, 3, 4] sts at beginning of next 2 rows, then dec 1 st, each side, of next and every following alternate row until 50 [52, 56, 58] sts remain. Continue to work evenly until armholes measure 2 inches (5 centimeters) [2¼ inches (5.75 centimeters), 2½ inches (6.25 centimeters), 2¾ inches (7 centimeters)] overall, ending with a p row.

Divide for back opening: K 22 [23, 25, 26] sts. Put remaining sts on holder. Turn work. Continue to work evenly in St st until armhole measures 4½ inches (11.5 centimeters) [5 inches (12.5 centimeters), 5½ inches (14 centimeters), 6 inches (15.25 centimeters)] from beginning of shaping. End at armhole edge.

Shape shoulder: Bind off 7 [7, 8, 8] sts at beginning of next row and 7 sts at beginning of following alternate row. Work 1 row. Bind off. Take sts off holder. With RS facing, sl first 6 sts onto safety pin. Join yarn to next st and k to end of row. Complete to match first side.

FRONT

Work as for back up to marker.

Dec row (RS): K4 [4, 8, 2]; *k 2 tog, k3 [3, 3, 4]; repeat from * to last 3 [7, 9, 4] sts; k 2 tog, k1 [5, 7, 2] (74 [78, 84, 90] sts).

1st ribbing row: K14 [12, 13, 16]; *p1, k2; repeat from * to last 15 [12, 14, 17] sts; p1, k to end.

2nd ribbing row: P14 [11, 13, 16]; *k1, p2; repeat from * to last 15 [13, 14, 17] sts; k1, p to end. Repeat these 2 rows once more; then work the 1st row again.

Shape armholes: Bind off 2 [3, 3, 4] sts at beginning of next 2 rows. Then dec 1 st, each side, of next row and then every other row until 58 [62, 64, 66] sts remain. Work evenly until armholes measure 3 inches (7.5 centimeters) [3½ inches (9 centimeters), 4 inches (10 centimeters), 4½ inches (11.5 centimeters)] from beginning of shaping. End with WS row.

Divide for neck: Work 23 [24, 25, 26] sts in pattern. Put remaining sts on holder. Turn work. Dec 1 st at neck edge every row until 16 [17, 17, 18] sts remain. Work evenly until front measures same as back to beginning of shoulder shaping, ending at armhole edge.

Shape armhole: Bind off 8 [9, 9, 9] sts at beg of next row. Work 1 row. Bind off. With RS facing, join another ball of yarn and bind off first 12 [14, 14, 14] sts. Work to end of row. Complete to match first side of neck.

SLEEVE

With medium-sized needles, cast on 36 [36, 38, 38] sts and work k1, p1 ribbing for 1½ inches (3.75 centimeters).

Inc row: Rib 4 [1, 2, 4] sts; *work twice into next st, rib 2 [2, 2, 1] sts; repeat from * to last 5 [2, 3, 4] sts; work twice into next st, rib to end (46 [48, 50, 54] sts). Change to larger needles. Work evenly in St st until sleeve measures 8 inches (20 centimeters) [9½ inches (24 centimeters), 10½ inches (26.5 centimeters), 11½ inches (29.25 centimeters)] overall. End with a p row. (Continued next page.)

NOTE: Length can be adjusted here.

Shape top: Bind off 2 [3, 3, 4] sts at beginning of next 2 rows. Dec 1 st, each side, next and every following 4th row until 30 [28, 30, 30] sts remain. Then dec 1 st, each side, every following alternate row until 26 [22, 18, 18] sts remain. Now dec 1 st, each side, every row, until 12 sts remain.

Bind off.

Work another sleeve in the same manner.

NECKBAND

Join shoulder seams. With RS facing, join yarn to left side for back neck, and, using medium-sized needles, pick up and k 8 [9, 10, 11] sts from left side of back neck, 11 sts down left front neck, 12 [14, 14, 14] sts at center front neck, 11 sts up right front neck, and 8 [9, 10, 11] sts from right side of back neck (50 [54, 56, 58] sts). Beginning with p row, work 3 rows St st.

Picot row: K1; *yo, k 2 tog; repeat from * to last st; k1. Beginning with p row, work 3 rows St st.

Bind off.

Fold neckband to WS and sew in place.

BUTTON BORDER

With largest needles, cast on 6 sts and work garter st until border, slightly stretched, fits up back neck opening to top of neck edging. Bind off. Sew border onto dress. Mark 4 button positions on border, the 1st one ½ inch (1.25 centimeters) from cast-on edge, the top one ½ inch (1.25 centimeters) from bound-off edge, and the others spaced evenly between.

BUTTONHOLE BORDER

Take 6 sts off safety pin. With RS facing, join on yarn and k these 6 sts.

Work border as for button border, but make buttonholes in line with button markers as follows:

Buttonhole row (RS): K2, k 2 tog, yo, k2. Sew border onto dress.

FINISHING

Run a thread around sleeve top and ease into armhole. Sew in place. Join side and sleeve seams. Turn up hem and sew in place. Sew on buttons.

Smocking: Using a contrasting color and beginning at side edge, smock bodice by taking alternate pairs of ridges tog and overcasting to secure. Alternate smocking rows 1½ inches (3.75 centimeters) apart. (See page 158.)

CHILD'S SNAKES AND LADDERS CARDIGAN

(Color photo page 40)

Wonderfully fierce monsters may be made from the tubes formed by spool-knitting, page 159. The wearer of this sweater may even be able to make the snakes and ladders himself or herself, to be appliquéd onto the cardigan after it is knitted.

SIZES: Child's 1 [3, 6, 8, 10]

MATERIALS:

Yarn: Emu Superwash wool (50-gram balls) of royal blue *(main color)* For the snakes, small amounts of emerald green, yellow, scarlet, and black and white (for eyes)

Needles: Straight knitting needles, U.S. sizes 3 and 5 (Continental sizes 3¼ and 4) *Or sizes needed to obtain gauge*

Notions: Stitch holders, tapestry needle, 6 buttons

GAUGE: With larger needles, in stockinette stitch, 12 stitches and 15 rows = 2 inches (5 centimeters)

FINISHED MEASUREMENTS:

Chest: 20 inches (50.75 centimeters) [22 inches (56 centimeters), 24 inches (61 centimeters), 26 inches (66 centimeters), 28 inches (71 centimeters)]

Sleeve (measured at underarm seam): 7½ inches (19 centimeters) [8 inches (20 centimeters), 9 inches (23 centimeters), 10 inches (25.5 centimeters), 11½ inches (29.25 centimeters)]

Length: 13 inches (33 centimeters) [14 inches (35.5 centimeters), 15½ inches (39.5 centimeters), 17 inches (43 centimeters), 18 inches (45.5 centimeters)]

BACK

With smaller needles and main color, cast on 61 [67, 73, 77, 83] sts and work k1, p1 ribbing for 1½ inches (3.75 centimeters). Change to larger needles. Work evenly in St st until back measures 8 inches (20 centimeters) [8½ inches (21.5 centimeters), 9½ inches (24 centimeters), 10½ inches (26.5

centimeters), 11½ inches (29.25 centimeters)] overall. End with p row.

Shape armholes: Bind off 3 [3, 4, 4, 5] sts at beginning of next 2 rows. Dec 1 st, each side, every following alternate row until 47 [51, 55, 57, 59] sts remain. Work evenly in St st until armholes measure 5 inches (12.5 centimeters) [5½ inches (14 centimeters), 5¾ inches (14.5 centimeters), 6¼ inches (16 centimeters), 6½ inches (16.5 centimeters)] from beginning of shaping. End with p row.

Shape shoulders: Bind off 6 [7, 8, 8, 8] sts at beginning of next 2 rows and 6 [6, 7, 7, 7] sts at beginning of following 2 rows. Bind off remaining sts.

FIRST FRONT (LEFT FOR BOY, RIGHT FOR GIRL)

Pocket lining: With larger needles and main color, cast on 13 [15, 17, 17, 17] sts and work in St st for 2 inches (5 centimeters). End with k row for a girl and p row for a boy. Cut off yarn. Put sts on holder.

With smaller needles and main color, cast on 31 [33, 37, 39, 41] sts and work k1, p1 ribbing for 1½ inches (3.75 centimeters). *For sizes 3 and 10 only,* inc 1 st at middle of last row of ribbing (31 [34, 37, 39, 42] sts). Change to larger needles. Work evenly in St st until front measures 8 inches (20 centimeters) [8½ inches (21.5 centimeters), 9½ inches (24 centimeters), 10½ inches (26.5 centimeters), 11½ inches (29.25 centimeters)] overall. End with p row for a boy and k row for a girl.

Shape armhole: Bind off 3 [3, 4, 4, 5] sts at beginning of next row. Dec 1 st at armhole edge, every following alternate row until 24 [26, 28, 29, 30]

sts remain. Work 5 [5, 5, 6, 6] rows St st. End at armhole edge.

Beginning 1st pocket row for boy and 2nd pocket row for girl, place pockets as follows:

1st pocket row: K5 [5, 5, 6, 6]; *p1, k1; repeat from * 5 [6, 7, 7, 7] times; p1; k to end.

2nd pocket row: P6 [6, 6, 6, 7]; *k1, p1; repeat from * 5 [6, 7, 7, 7] times; k1; p to end. Repeat last 2 rows 1 [1, 2, 2, 2] times more. For girl only, work 1 more row.

Next row: Work 5 [5, 5, 6, 6] sts; bind off in ribbing next 13 [15, 17, 17, 17] sts; work to end of row.

Next row: Work 6 [6, 6, 6, 7] sts; work pocket lining sts; work to end of row.

Continue to work evenly in St st until armhole measures 3½ inches (9 centimeters) [4 inches (10 centimeters), 4 inches (10 centimeters), 4½ inches (11.5 centimeters), 4½ inches (11.5 centimeters)] from beginning of shaping. End at front edge.

Shape neck: Bind off 6 [7, 7, 8, 8] sts at beg of next row. Dec 1 st at neck edge, every row, until 12 [13, 15, 15, 15] sts remain. Work evenly in St st until armhole measures same as back up to shoulder shaping, ending at armhole edge.

Shape shoulder: Bind off 6 [7, 8, 8, 8] sts at beginning of next row. Work 1 row. Bind off.

SECOND FRONT (RIGHT FOR BOY, LEFT FOR GIRL)

With smaller needles and main color, cast on 31 [33, 37, 39, 41] sts and work k1, p1 ribbing for 1½ inches (3.75 centimeters). *For sizes 3 and 10 only,* inc 1 st at middle of last row of ribbing (31 [34, 37, 39, 42] sts). Change to larger needles. For boy, work 2 rows St st. For girl, work 3 rows St st. End at front edge.

Place pocket: Work 24 sts. Put remaining sts on holder. Turn work. Work evenly in St st for 3½ inches (9 centimeters) [4 inches (10 centimeters), 4 inches (10 centimeters), 4½ inches (11.5 centimeters), 4½ inches (11.5 centimeters)], ending at inner edge. Cut off yarn. Leave sts on a 2nd holder.

Return to sts on 1st holder. Join on yarn. Cast on 17 sts inner edge. Work across these 17 sts and then work the 7 [10, 13, 15, 18] sts (24 [27, 30, 32, 35] sts). Continue working evenly in St st for 3½ inches (9 centimeters) [4 inches (10 centimeters), 4 inches (10 centimeters), 4½ inches (11.5 centimeters), 4½ inches (11.5 centimeters)], ending at inner edge.

Next row: Bind off 17 sts, work to end of row.

Next row: Work 7 [10, 13, 15, 18] sts, then work the 24 sts from 2nd holder (31 [34, 37, 39, 42] sts). Continue working evenly in St st until front measures 8 inches (20 centimeters) [8½ inches (21.5 centimeters), 9½ inches (24 centimeters), 10½ inches (26.5 centimeters), 11½ inches (29.25 centimeters)] overall, ending at side edge.

Shape armhole: Bind off 3 [3, 4, 4, 5] sts at beginning of next row. Then dec 1 st, at armhole edge, next and every following alternate row until 24 [26, 28, 29, 30] sts remain. Continue working evenly in St st until armhole measures 3½ inches (9 centimeters) [4 inches (10 centimeters), 4 inches (10 centimeters), 4½ inches (11.5 centimeters), 4½ inches (11.5 centimeters)] from beginning of

shaping, ending at front edge. Shape neck same as first front and work until same length as first front to shoulder shaping.

Shape shoulder: Bind off 6 [7, 8, 8, 8] sts at beginning of next row. Work 1 row. Bind off.

Pocket edge: With RS facing, join on main color and, with smaller needles, pick up and k 21 [23, 23, 25, 25] sts along straight edge of pocket. Beginning with 2nd row, work k1, p1 ribbing for 1 inch (2.5 centimeters). Bind off in ribbing.

SLEEVE

With smaller needles and main color, cast on 34 [34, 36, 36, 38] sts and work k1, p1 ribbing for 1½ inches (3.75 cm). Change to larger needles. Working in St st, inc 1 st, each side, next and every following 7th [7th, 6th, 6th, 7th] row until 44 [46, 50, 52, 56] sts remain. Continue working evenly in St st until sleeve measures 7½ inches (18.75 centimeters) [8 inches (20 centimeters), 9 inches (23 centimeters), 10 inches (25.5 centimeters), 11½ inches (29.25 centimeters)] overall. End with p row.

Shape top: Bind off 3 [3, 4, 4, 5] sts at beginning of next 2 rows. Dec 1 st, each side, next and every following 4th row until 34 [34, 36, 38, 40] sts remain. Then dec 1 st, each side, every row, until 10 sts remain.

Bind off and work another sleeve in the same manner.

NECKBAND

Join shoulder seams. With RS facing, join main color to right front neck, and, with smaller needles, pick up and k 16 [18, 20, 22, 24] sts up right side of front neck, 23 [25, 25, 27, 29] sts from back neck, and 16 [18, 20, 22, 24] sts down left side of front neck (55 [61, 65, 71, 77] sts).

Beginning with 2nd row, work k1, p1 ribbing for 1 inch (2.5 centimeters). Bind off in ribbing.

BUTTON BORDER

With smaller needles and main color, cast on 9 sts and work k1, p1 ribbing until border, slightly stretched, fits up front to top of neckband. Bind off. Sew border to front. Mark 6 button positions on this border, the 1st one ½ inch (1.25 centimeters) from cast-on edge, the top one ½ inch from bound-off edge, and the others spaced evenly between.

BUTTONHOLE BORDER

Work as for button border, but make buttonholes to correspond to button positions, as follows:

Buttonhole row (RS): K1, p1, k1, p1, yo, p 2 tog, k1, p1, k1.

Sew border to other front.

FINISHING

Set in sleeves, then join side and sleeve seams. Sew pocket ends and pocket lining in position. Sew on buttons where marked.

TRIMMINGS

Delightful snakes may be made by spool-knitting (see page 159). To knit, proceed as follows: With smaller needles and contrasting color, cast on 20 sts, then bind them off. Make 5 more snakes. Embroider eyes on 3 snakes. Sew these into top pocket. Sew remaining 3 snakes into lower pocket. Embroider ladder up to top pocket.

CHILD'S HUMPTY-DUMPTY SWEATER
(Color photo page 41)

Humpty-Dumpty is as much fun for a child to wear as it is for you to knit. The "wall" is done in honeycomb stitch (see page 101). Humpty is knitted separately and then sewn on—both back and front!

SIZES: Child's 6 months [1, 3, 6, 8]

MATERIALS:
Yarn: Emu Superwash wool (50-gram balls)
    3 balls of yellow *(A)*
    1 ball of white *(B)*
    1 ball of black *(C)*
    Small amounts of scarlet *(D),* tan *(E),* and royal blue *(F)*
Needles: Straight knitting needles, U.S. sizes 3 and 5 (Continental sizes 3¼ and 4)
    Or sizes needed to obtain gauge
Notions: Tapestry needle, 1 button, padding or batting for Humpty-Dumpty

GAUGE: With larger needles, in stockinette stitch, 11 stitches and 15 rows = 2 inches (5 centimeters)

FINISHED MEASUREMENTS:
Chest: 18 inches (45.5 centimeters) [20 inches (50.75 centimeters), 22 inches (56 centimeters), 24 inches (61 centimeters), 26 inches (66 centimeters)]
Sleeve (measured at underarm seam): 7 inches (17.75 centimeters) [7½ inches (19 centimeters), 8 inches (20 centimeters), 9 inches (23 centimeters), 10½ inches (26.5 centimeters)]
Length: 11 inches (28 centimeters) [12 inches (30.5 centimeters), 13½ inches

(34.25 centimeters), 15 inches (38 centimeters), 16 inches (40.5 centimeters)]

BACK

With smaller needles and color A, cast on 55 [63, 67, 75, 79] sts and work k1, p1 ribbing for 1½ inches (4 centimeters). Cut off color A. Join on colors B and C. Change to larger needles. Proceed in brick pattern, as follows:

ROWS 1 AND 2: K with color B.

ROW 3: K1 color C; *sl 1 purlwise, k3 color C; repeat from * to last 2 sts; sl 1 purlwise, p1 color C.

ROW 4: P1 color C; *sl 1, k3 color C; repeat from * to last 2 sts; sl 1; p1 color C.

ROWS 5 AND 6: K with color B.

ROW 7: K3 color C; *sl 1 purlwise, k3 color C; repeat from * to end.

ROW 8: P3 color C; *sl 1, p3 color C; repeat from * to end.

Repeat these 8 rows 2 [2, 3, 4, 4] times more. Then work 1st through 6th rows again. Cut off colors B and C. Join on colors A and D. Twisting yarn at back of work to avoid making holes, proceed as follows:

ROW 1 (RS): K15 [19, 21, 25, 27] color A; k28 color D; join on a second ball of color A and k to end.

ROW 2: P13 [17, 19, 23, 25] color A; p26 color D; p to end with color A.

ROW 3: K16 [20, 22, 26, 28] color A; k26 color D; k to end with color A.

ROW 4: P14 [18, 20, 24, 26] color A; p24 color D; p to end with color A.

ROW 5: K18 [22, 24, 28, 30] color A; k22 color D; k to end with color A.

ROW 6: P16 [20, 22, 26, 28] color A; p20 color D; p to end with color A.

ROW 7: K20 [24, 26, 30, 32] color A; k18 color D; k to end with color A.

ROW 8: P19 [23, 25, 29, 31] color A; p14 color D; p to end with color A.

ROW 9: K23 [27, 29, 33, 35] color A; k12 color D; k to end with color A.

ROW 10: P22 [26, 28, 32, 34] color A; p8 color D; p to end with color A.

Cut off color D and 2nd ball of color A. With color A only, work in St st until back measures 7 inches (17.75 centimeters) [7½ inches (19 centimeters), 8½ inches (21.5 centimeters), 9½ inches (24 centimeters), 10 inches (25.5 centimeters)] overall. End with p row.

Shape raglan: Bind off 3 sts at beginning of next 2 rows. Dec 1 st, each side, next row. Work 3 [1, 3, 1, 3] rows. Then dec 1 st, each side, next and every following alternate row until 21 [23, 25, 27, 29] sts remain, ending p row. Cut off yarn. Put sts on holder.

FRONT

With smaller needles and color A, cast on 55 [63, 67, 75, 79] sts and work k1, p1 ribbing for 1½ inches (3.75 centimeters). Cut off color A. Join on colors B and C. Change to larger needles. Proceed in brick pattern, as follows:

ROWS 1 AND 2: K with color B.

ROW 3: K1 color C, *sl 1 purlwise, p3 color C; repeat from * to last 2 sts; sl 1 purlwise, p1 color C.

ROW 4: P1 color C; *sl 1, k3 color C; repeat from * to last 2 sts; sl 1; p1 color C.

ROWS 5 AND 6: K with color B.

ROW 7: K3 color C; *sl 1 purlwise, k3 color C; repeat from * to end.

ROW 8: P3 color C; *sl 1, p3 color C; repeat from * to end.

Repeat these 8 rows 2 [2, 3, 4, 4] times more. Then work Rows 1–6 again. Cut off colors B and C. Join on color A. Work St st until front measures 7 inches (17.75 centimeters) [7½ inches (19 centimeters), 8½ inches (21.5 centimeters), 9½ inches (24 centimeters), 10 inches (25.5 centimeters)] overall. End with p row.

Shape raglan: Bind off 3 sts at beginning of next 2 rows. Dec 1 st, each side, next row. Work 3 [1, 3, 1, 3] rows. Then dec 1 st, each side, next and every following alternate row until 35 [37, 41, 43, 45] sts remain, ending p row.

Divide for neck: K 2 tog, k10 [10, 12, 12, 12]. Put remaining sts on holder.

Turn work. Dec 1 st, each side, every following alternate row, until 3 sts remain, ending p row. Dec 1 st at raglan on next row. P 1 row. K 2 tog; fasten off. Return to sts on holder. With RS facing, sl 1st 11 [13, 13, 15, 17] sts onto holder. Join yarn to next st. K to last 2 sts; k 2 tog. Complete to match 1st side of neck.

SLEEVE

With smaller needles and color A, cast on 34 [34, 36, 38, 38] sts and work k1, p1 ribbing for 1½ inches (3.75 centimeters).

Change to larger needles. Work in St st. *At the same time,* inc 1 st, each side, 3rd and every following 6th row, until there are 44 [46, 50, 52, 56] sts. Continue working in St st until sleeve measures 7 inches (17.75 centimeters) [7½ inches (19 centimeters), 8½ inches (21.5 centimeters), 9½ inches (23.75 centimeters), 10 inches (25.5 centimeters)] overall. End with p row.

Shape raglan: Bind off 3 sts at beginning of next 2 rows.
Dec 1 st, each side, end of next and every following 4th row 1 [2, 2, 3, 3] times (34 [34, 38, 38, 42] sts).
P 1 row.
Dec 1 st, each side, next and every following alternate row until 10 sts remain, ending with p row. Cut off yarn. Put sts on holder.
Work another sleeve in the same manner.

Neckband: With RS facing, join color A to sts of first sleeve. With smaller needles, k sts from holder; pick up and k 13 [13, 14, 14, 15] sts down left side of front neck, k front neck sts from holder, pick up and k 13 [13, 14, 14, 15] sts up right side of front neck, k the second sleeve sts and back neck sts from holder (78 [82, 86, 90,

96] sts). Work 5 rows in k1, p1 ribbing.
Bind off in ribbing.

FINISHING

Join neckband and raglan seams. Join side and sleeve seams.

Humpty-Dumpty: With larger needles and color D, cast on 9 sts. Work in St st. *At the same time,* inc 1 st, each side, every row, until there are 19 sts; then inc 1 st, each side, every following alternate row until there are 25 sts. End with p row. Cut off color D. Join on color B. Work 4 rows St st. Cut off color B. Join on color E. Dec 1 st, each side, next and every following 4th row until 19 sts remain; then dec 1 st, each side, every row, until 11 sts remain. End with p row.
Next row: K 3 tog, k to last 3 sts, k 3 tog (7 sts). Bind off.
Arms: Using larger needles and color D, cast on 5 sts. Work 6 rows St st. Cut off color D. Join on color B. K 2 rows. Cut off color B. Join on color E. Work 6 rows St st. Bind off. Make 2 more arms the same way.
Hand: With larger needles and color E, cast on 5 sts. Work 6 rows St st. Bind off.
1st leg: With larger needles and color F, cast on 6 sts. Work 12 rows St st.
Next row: Cast on 3 sts; join on color D; *k1 color F, k1 color D; repeat from *; k4 color F; k1 color D.
Next row: P2 color D, p2 color F, p2 color D, P1 color F, p1 color D, p twice into last st using color F.
Next row: K2 color F, k1 color D, k1 color F, k6 color D. Cut off color F.
Next row: P9, p twice into last st (11 sts). K 1 row. Continuing in St st, dec 1 st, each side, next and following 2 alternate rows. Dec 1 st, each side, next row. Bind off.

Make 2 more in the same way.
2nd leg: Work as for 1st leg, reversing the shaping. Make 2 more in the same way.
To complete Humpty-Dumpty: Sew 2 single arms to body.
Front design: Sew 2 pairs matching legs together (1 each 1st leg and 2nd leg). With colors B, C, and D, embroider eyes, nose, mouth, and curl. Sew body and legs in position, leaving opening for padding. Insert padding. Sew opening closed.
Bow tie: With larger needles and color C, cast on 22 sts. K 7 rows. Bind off. Join short seam and fold in half, seam line at center. Gather at center, then sew in place.
Back design: Sew remaining single legs in position. Sew arms and hand in position. Sew on button.

BLOCKING AND CARING FOR YOUR SWEATER

Now that you have completed your sweater fabric, it is time to assemble it (see page 171). Proper finishing makes all the difference to the finished sweater. Before rushing to sew it together—because you can't wait to see the end product—be patient and block it. You will be pleased with the professional results.

Cover a board with plastic and over that stretch several layers of toweling. Cover the toweling layer with a sheet. Pin your sweater pieces into shape, placing pins at right angles to the sweater edge. Next, cover the sweater piece with a layer of dampened toweling. Allow it to dry in its own time.

Nowadays, many yarns need little blocking. For this reason, it may be quite sufficient simply to steam your sweater. To do this, lay the sweater flat on the ironing board and cover with a cloth. Use a lot of steam and hold the iron above the sweater, pressing lightly only the seams. Alternatively, the carpet is an ideal surface—it has the effect of Velcro. If you wish, throw a terry cloth towel down first and then use T-pins to stretch the sweater into shape. Cover it with a wet cloth, steam it with the steam iron, and allow it to dry completely—still pinned out. *Never* block or steam acrylic sweaters. Man-made fibers may lose their elasticity and may be ruined forever by pressing.

LAUNDERING

With careful handling, your hand-knit, natural-yarn sweater can last through many washings. Wash in cool or lukewarm water, using pure soap. Squeeze gently. Avoid handling too much. You may have to wash several times, but *never* change the temperature of the water. Rinse well, again at the same temperature. Squeeze, shake, and roll up in a clean, dry terry cloth towel. Roll tightly and pound the roll to remove excess moisture quickly. Unroll, shake, and lay out another dry towel to dry, away from direct heat and sunlight—preferably with ventilation above and below. (Drying racks are available in most hardware stores.) Smooth the sweater out to restore shape, and shake and fluff it from time to time during the drying process. This should remove all creases. If there are any left, follow the steam process described above.

CARE

To avoid stretching, never hang your sweater on a coat hanger.

Never store your sweater in plastic—it needs to breathe.

Newspaper is an excellent moth preventive.

ANGORA

When knitting angora, place a towel across your lap to prevent furry clotting.

Wash beaded angora sweaters by hand as described above. Do not dry-clean.

If angora is flattened, spruce it up by brushing with a hairbrush.

Cut down on angora shedding by placing angora sweaters in the freezer for about one hour before wearing.

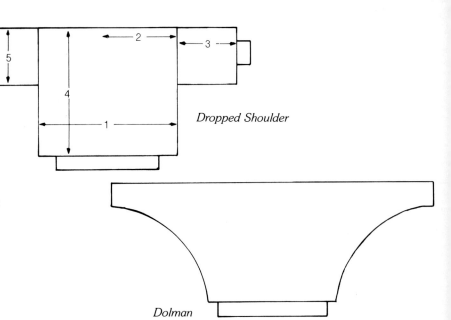

Dropped Shoulder

Dolman

TAKING YOUR MEASUREMENTS

To adjust a sweater pattern or create your own, you need to know how to take your measurements. First you must decide on your sweater shape, because this determines how you will measure. Although there are many variations in neck, sleeve, and body shapes, the two basic ways of taking measurements are for set-in sleeves and for dolman (or dropped-shoulder) sleeves.

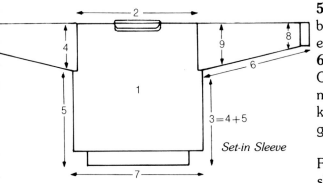

Set-in Sleeve

To Take Measurements for Set-in Sleeve Style (Puff or Plain)

1. Bust
2. Shoulder to shoulder
3. Shoulder to bottom
4. Armhole size
5. Underarm to bottom
6. Underarm to wrist
7. Waist
8. Around wrist
9. Around upper arm

To Take Measurements for Dolman or Dropped-Shoulder Styles

1. Center neck to wrist.
2. Front body.
3. Divide measurement 2 in half and subtract answer from measurement 1.
4. Measurement 3 gives sleeve length. For dropped shoulder, loose-fitting style,

do not measure underarm; it does not give correct fit.

5. Shoulder to desired length (waist or below). Add 1 inch (2.5 centimeters) for ease.
6. Around upper arm.

Once you have taken your measurements, draw out your pattern on knitter's graph paper. One square of the grid can equal 1 inch (2.5 centimeters).

For a fitted, set-in sleeve, you will need shaping.

Armhole: Acute at first, the armhole shaping may be gradual after the first 2 or 3 inches, resulting in a gradual curve to the shoulder.

Shoulder: Start shaping approximately 1 inch (2.5 centimeters) before the finished length of the sweater is reached, binding off in three to four long steps to make a gradual slant.

Neck: Front neck shaping usually begins 2 inches (5 centimeters) below center back neck. Divide the stitches at the center point and work both together, decreasing evenly at neck edge until shoulder shaping reaches the same measurement as back edge.

Sleeves: As at waist, increase in the final row of ribbing, then continue to increase both sides to form a smooth, slanting line up to the armhole.

THINGS YOU NEED TO KNOW

JOINING When edges have been neatly finished by slipping the first stitch of every row (see page 173), the edges may be joined easily by oversewing, or by backstitching as shown, or by laying the edges side by side and sliding the needle from one side to the other. Use a blunt tapestry needle to avoid splitting threads. Some professional finishers place right sides together and join seams by machine stitching just the fabric. This results in a fine invisible seam. If the stitches are loopy, cover them with tissue, which can be torn away afterward. This will allow the foot of the machine to slide on top easily.

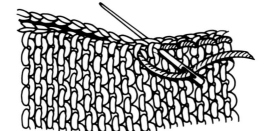

Back Stitch

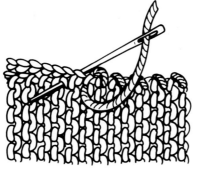

Overcast Stitch

JOINING AS YOU KNIT Joining two pieces together can be achieved quite simply by knitting them together off both needles simultaneously. This is an excellent method of joining shoulder seams.

Hold the two needles together, right sides facing. With a third needle, slip through the first stitch on the front needle *and* the first stitch on the back needle. Knit the two together.

As you work, bind off the stitches in the usual manner (see page 32).

UNRAVELING If you have several rows to correct, slide the needle out and pull the yarn carefully, unraveling as needed. Pick up the stitches and continue knitting. If you have only one row to unpick, pick up the stitches of the previous row one by one. Slip the needle into each loop of the row below, allowing the top stitch to drop off as you go. Pick up the stitches as they fall on the needle. If they are fighting you, correct them on the first row you knit. Stitches should be open at the bottom and should not cross. To correct stitches, simply take them up on the right needle and turn them around, or knit into the back instead of the front of each stitch.

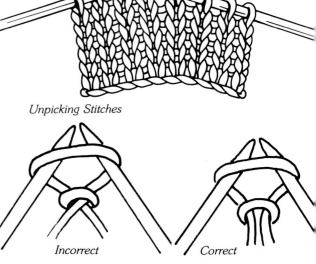

Unpicking Stitches

Incorrect   *Correct*

172

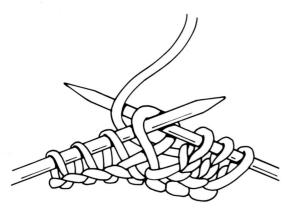

FORMING A FIRM CAST-ON
EDGE To form a firm edge at the bottom of your garment, cast on the required number of stitches. Then knit into the back of each stitch on the first row.

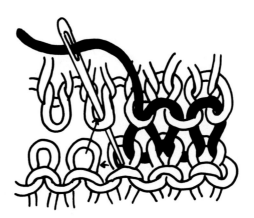

GRAFTING A means of joining two pieces that have been unraveled or knit with invisible cast-on. Use a tapestry needle and weave as in diagram.

CABLE CAST-ON Similar to a knit cast-on except the stitch is worked in the space between the stitches rather than through the stitch itself. When beginning the first row, knit into the front of the stitch for a sturdy braidlike selvedge.

INVISIBLE CAST-ON This is an excellent method of casting on when you don't want to see the selvedge, such as when you will be sewing one piece onto another or if two pieces are to be joined at the edge. To do this, wrap the yarn around the needle and a scrap thread, as in the diagram. When the stitching is complete, pull out the scrap thread and you are left with a row of loops.

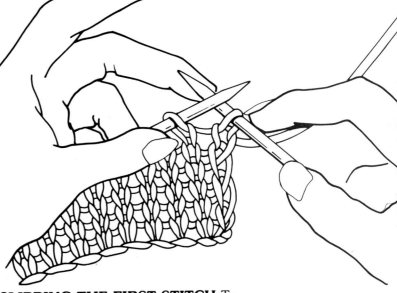

SLIPPING THE FIRST STITCH To form a neat side edge, instead of knitting, slip the first stitch of each row. That is, take the loop from the left needle onto the right without knitting it. This firm, braided edge makes joining pieces of knitting easy.

COUNTING ROWS If stitches are hard to count, turn the work horizontally and count each row. For example, 12 rows equal 6 stitches.

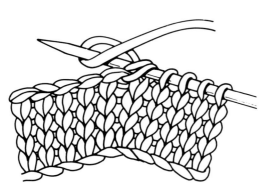

PICKING UP STITCHES FROM A BOUND-OFF NECK EDGE

Plan ahead to be sure that the stitches you pick up will be evenly spaced around the neckline. Place a marker every 2 inches (5 centimeters) around the neckline. Divide the number of stitches you need to pick up by the number of marked-off areas. The answer tells you how many stitches you should pick up in each marked-off area to keep picked-up stitches evenly spaced.

If your pattern does not tell you how many stitches to pick up, the rule of thumb is one stitch for every bound-off stitch. Be sure to pick up the correct multiple of stitches to make your pattern come out evenly. For example, if you are going to work k2, p2 ribbing on your picked-up stitches, the number of stitches you pick up should be divisible by 4.

To pick up stitches, work with the right side of the garment facing you. Begin by inserting the needle front-to-back in the bound-off stitch, going under both strands of the loop of the bound-off stitch. Wind the yarn you are using for your collar or neckband around the needle as if to knit a stitch, and bring a loop through to the right side of the work. Keep the loop on the needle and go on to the next stitch to be picked up. Repeat all around the neckline, and you are ready to go. Work the next row from the wrong side and continue in the desired pattern.

If your collar or neckband is in stockinette stitch and is a different color from the stitches you are picking up from, make the picked-up stitches in the original color and switch to the new color on the next row.

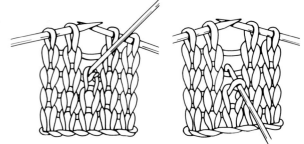

DROPPED STITCHES

It is easiest to pick up dropped stitches with a crochet hook.

SHORTENING OR LENGTHENING AT RIBBING

Pull the thread right across knitting until a clear line shows. Snip the pulled thread at the edge, and carefully draw the thread from the opposite edge across the work. The knitting will separate, leaving a clear row of loops exposed which may then be picked up to knit the ribbing.

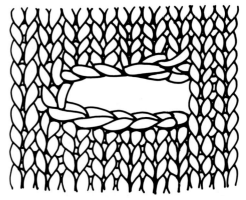

BUTTONHOLE

To form a buttonhole, cast off the number of stitches required to fit the button (*fewer* than it appears, since knitting is stretchy). On the next row, cast on again and continue to knit.

BODY MEASUREMENT CHARTS

Infants and Children (boys and girls)

Size	6 mo	1	2	3	4	5	6	7	8	10	12	14
Chest	19	20	21	22	23	23½	24	25	26	28	30	32
Waist	19	19½	20	20½	21	21½	22	22½	23	24	25	26
Hip						25	26	27	28	30	32½	35
Back Waist Length								11	11½	12½	13	13¾
Sleeve Length	6	7	8	8¾	9½	10¾	11	11½	12	13½	14½	16

Misses and Women

Size	8	10	12	14	16	18	20	22
Bust	31½	32½	34	36	38	40	42	44
Waist	24	25	26½	28	30	32	34	36
Hip	33½	34½	36	38	40	42	44	46
Back Waist Length	15¾	16	16¼	16½	16¾	17	17-1/8	17¼
Sleeve Length	16¼	16½	17	17½	18	18	18	18

Women's Half Sizes

Size	10½	12½	14½	16½	18½	20½
Bust	33	35	37	39	41	43
Waist	27	29	31	33	35	37
Hip	37	39	41	43	45	47
Back Waist Length	15¼	15½	15¾	16	16¼	16½

Men

Chest	32	34	36	38	40	42	44
Waist	28	30	32	34	36	38	40

SUPPLIERS

The sweaters on pages 76, 96, 114, 121, and 150 by Anny Blatt Yarns, 24770 Crestview Court, Farmington Hills, MI 48331, may be knitted in alternate yarns as follows:
Starblitz—Super kid, Jaspé (two strands together); for
Honeymoon—Lazur, Canberra, Melbourne, Adelaide; for
Bright'Anny—Canberra. The sweater on page 66 is available from Ragamuffin, Armadale Pier, Sleat, Isle of Skye, Scotland. The sweater on page 102 was worked in pure silk from the Sheepish Grin, 40 Fairfield Road, Kingston, NJ 08528. The sweaters on pages 70, 108, and 127 were worked in Lion Brand yarns from the Lion Brand Yarn Company, 34 West 15th Street, New York, NY 10011. The children's sweaters on pages 82, 83, 86, 98, 154, 160, 163, and 166 were worked in Emu yarn from Robin Wools, Emu International, Leeds Roads, Idle Bradford, West Yorkshire, Great Britain; available in the United States from the Plymouth Yarn Company, P.O. Box 28, Lafayette Street, Brystol, PA 19007. A selection of the above, including the Sheep and Hearts, Bobbles and Bands, Evening Rose, Tyrolean, and Nantucket sweaters are also available in kits from Erica Wilson Needleworks, 717 Madison Avenue, New York, NY 10021, (212) 832-7290.

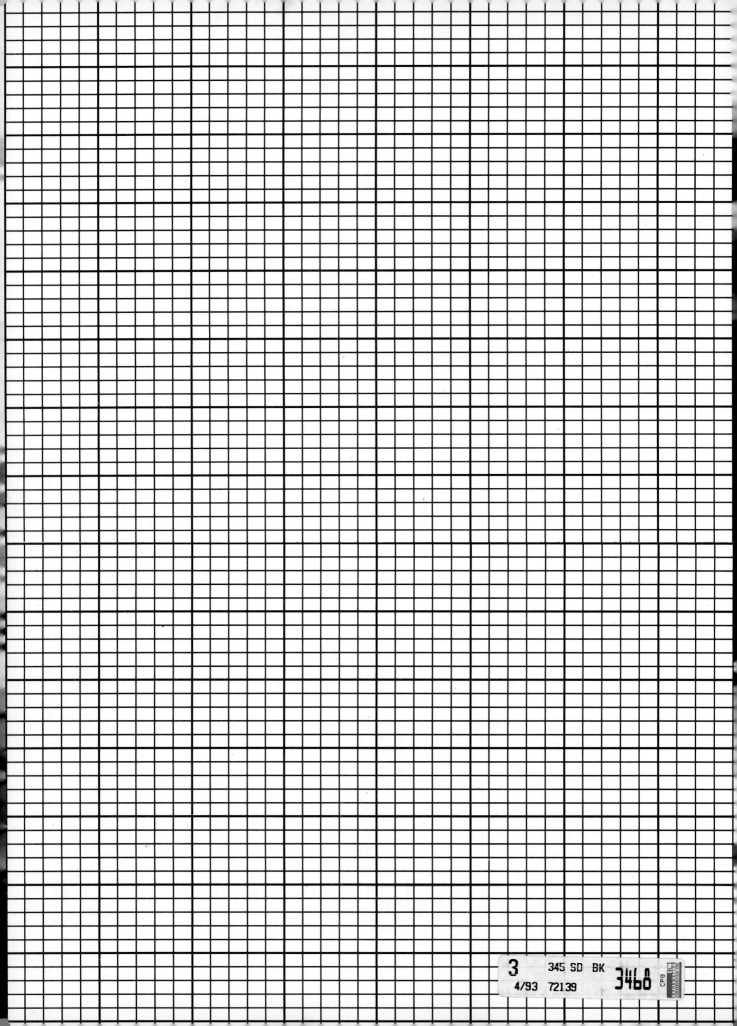